Contents

Foreword

Teaching in higher education is a very private business even when it is conducted in front of several hundred students. While there is often a great deal of discussion in staff rooms about academic issues, when it comes to teaching, discussion focuses on little more than anecdotes about particular students who may have caused irritation. Discourse and learning about the art of teaching are lamentably absent in most departments.

While there are many reasons for this state of affairs, there will never be a significant improvement in what we do unless we subject what occurs in the classroom and lecture hall to scrutiny and analysis. Without this each one of us may be forever destined to invent solutions to what, for all we know, may be common problems. To open up the teaching act to examination is profoundly challenging. Teachers in higher education are not used to being observed; they are not used to regarding teaching as a matter which can be discussed sensibly and improved systematically. The quaint idea that teachers are born and not made still prevails in too many quarters.

That is rapidly changing. In recent years, there has been a substantial shift of expectations concerning learning about teaching in higher education. Student evaluation of teaching is commonplace and courses for new entrants to the profession are becoming the norm rather than the exception. This is as it should be, but the change has left us with a dearth of good quality material which is suitable for use in learning about teaching. There are excellent books of advice (McKeachie, 1986), summaries of the literature (Brown and Atkins, 1988), and suggested checklists and activities (Gibbs and Habeshaw, 1989). What we do not have is material which has the scent of the classroom about it, which conjures up for us a situation that seems all too real, and which gives us the rush of adrenalin we feel when confronted by 'one of those students'.

While it is important for us to know about what research says and what excellent teachers would advise us to do, we also need to learn to think like skilled teachers and reflect upon our own practices. It is through developing reflective practice that we can lay the foundation for our own improvement.

There are many paths towards developing reflective practice. The starting point can be the study of our own activities through noticing what we do when we teach; it can be prompted by videotaping and replaying the action, by experienced colleagues sitting in on our classes, or by other devices which confront us with critical incidents about our teaching. While these activities are very worthwhile, they can be quite daunting. They can also limit us to our own experience and trap us in our existing perspective.

Peter Schwartz and Graham Webb have recognized the problem and over a number of years they have been developing ways of moving colleagues beyond their experience and what they observe around them into new worlds of practice. They do this through story telling. The stories are real and present incidents which are problematic and have been confronted by teachers in their normal day-to-day activities. Through reading and reflecting on these stories, presented in the form of case studies, teachers can begin to explore a repertoire of behaviours which they might deploy in similar or related situations.

Although the case studies in this book have been designed to be read and reflected upon by individuals, there are many other ways of using these case studies effectively, and most can be enhanced by discussion with groups of sympathetic colleagues. In an appendix to the book, Peter and Graham have given details of a discussion-based approach which works well in their context.

I have seen such a case study approach to academic staff development work well at Harvard for the unique teaching context there (Christensen, 1987) and have wondered how it might be applied to fit the more familiar higher education institutions in which most of us work. Peter Schwartz and Graham Webb show the way and provide a stimulus for the creation of many more cases to reflect the increasing diversity of post-secondary teaching. Now the research-based knowledge on teaching and learning in higher education can begin to be married to the rich context of day-to-day practice.

David Boud
Professor of Adult Education and
Head, School of Adult and Language Education,
University of Technology, Sydney.
November, 1992.

References

Brown, G and Atkins, M (1988) *Effective Teaching in Higher Education*, London: Methuen.

Christensen, C Roland (1987) *Teaching and the Case Method*, Boston, MA: Harvard Business School.

Gibbs, G and Habeshaw, T (1989) *Preparing to Teach. An Introduction to Effective Teaching in Higher Education*, Bristol: Technical and Educational Services.

McKeachie, W J (1986) *Teaching Tips. A Guidebook for the Beginning College Teacher*, 8th edn, Lexington, MA: D C Heath.

Acknowledgements

Firstly and most importantly, we extend our sincerest thanks to the higher education teachers who participated in the seminar series during which the case studies in this book were developed. Whether your cases are included in this book or not, your contributions were extremely valuable.

We thank John Bowden, Sally Brown, Mike O'Neil, and John Jones for their involvement in earlier stages of the project. We would also like to express our special appreciation of Dave Boud, for his encouragement and valuable guidance.

Graham Webb wishes to thank the University of Otago for granting the sabbatical leave which accelerated the completion of this project. He also wishes to thank Professor Gordon Bell and the Faculty of Education at Nottingham Trent University for their support during his sabbatical leave and as the book was completed. Thanks too to George and Prue for providing a home base and to Susan, Alan and Lauren for their usual, remarkable toleration of hours which should have been spent with them.

Peter Schwartz is extremely grateful to Arleen for putting up with his spending evenings and weekends writing and editing instead of being sociable.

Kogan Page and particularly Dolores Black have been efficient and decisive at all times. We are grateful for their professionalism and support.

Finally, we wish to acknowledge our colleagues in the Higher Education Development Centre at Otago. Terry Crooks has encouraged us and has provided every material support for this project from the time of its inception through to completion. Both Val Walton and Terry have suffered the authors' interminable project meetings in good grace. Sara Keen has battled through style changes and page re-numberings, sometimes concealed in cryptic fax and Email messages. To all of you, thanks.

Introduction

Why a book of case studies on teaching?

- *The student then leaned back in his chair and announced to the assembled group that he had done absolutely no work for the essay ... and had made the whole essay up. He went on to say that although the previous student had done far more work than he had, Simon had given a much lower mark....*

- *On the last day of lectures, Richard concluded his lecture and was about to pack up when Violet approached him. 'Are we supposed to learn everything for the exams with no indication as to what is more important?' she asked.*
  'Yes,' Richard replied.
  'Do you think that's reasonable?'
  'Yes,' he said again.
  'Well, I'd just like to tell you that I think your lecturing style is quite unsuitable.... I must have sat here for 50 hours and I've got less than five hours' worth of Planning Law. I'm sick of sitting listening to other students making up excuses for not preparing or avoiding the question. I just wanted you to know.'

- *Near the end of the session, Professor Edgley became defensive. He raised his voice and told the group that the 'facts' were as they were in the textbook and as he and other senior teachers had taught them. He said that Samuel was only a junior staff member and therefore inexperienced, whereas he was a professor.... One of the group asked: 'What do we need to know for the examination?' Edgley's response was immediate: 'The facts. What is in your textbook. You need not worry about what Samuel has told you as he will not be an examiner.'*

These are extracts from three of the case studies which appear in this book. Simon, Richard and Samuel are ordinary teachers who have found themselves confronted with difficult decisions to make concerning their teaching and relationships with students and colleagues. When you next meet them and the other teachers whose stories are told in the book, you will learn something of the background and circumstances which led to these incidents. You will be invited to put yourself in the teacher's place and to consider what *you* would have done had you been the teacher. By doing so, you will have the opportunity to learn something about yourself as a teacher and even, perhaps, something about yourself more generally, as a person. We believe that there is much for us all to learn about becoming better teachers, from reflecting upon the experience of teaching. As Martin (1981) has put it:

> Perhaps the best way to learn to teach these days is not to read the how-to handbooks but, rather, to have teachers describe their teaching.... Such descriptions, based on experience and reflection, may be the best instruction available to the newcomer. There are so few opportunities for teachers to observe other teachers teaching, or even to talk with them about teaching, that it is necessary to turn to secondary sources of information. And these reports, coming directly from the teachers, are so vital and relevant that they achieve a primary importance (p. 153).

We agree.

There are many very useful books on teaching which give numerous guidelines on how to teach well. However, such handbooks tend to give the impression that once teachers have the techniques right, they will not encounter further problems. Most of us know that is not true and that all sorts of unexpected problems arise in teaching. This book is about these sorts of problems. It presents case studies for you to consider, with the intention that you think about how and why the problems arose, and what could be done about them. *Unlike* a teaching handbook, this book's intention is not to be overly prescriptive. Instead, we hope to raise awareness; to provoke, promote, and provide insight; and to stimulate thought and reflection upon many important but frequently neglected aspects of the teacher's role.

As teachers in higher education, we are faced every day with decisions to make concerning the ways in which we teach and our relationships with students and colleagues. We usually rationalize the decisions we make from a fairly hazy world view concerning human nature, our ability to control our own destiny, and a conception of what teaching is all about. For example, we may view students as essentially lazy and needing to be forced to learn a prescribed syllabus by completing rigidly controlled assessment tasks. Conversely, we may see them as enthusiastic and competent learners who are eager to explore areas in which they themselves are interested. There are many more views of students and metaphors of teaching, some of which are evident in the case studies which follow. In each case study, the intention is to place you, the teacher, in situations which other teachers have actually experienced. You can then assess how well the teacher in the case responded to a difficult situation, what alternative responses were possible, how *you* would have acted if you had been in the teacher's place, and what implications the case has for your own teaching. As you do this, we hope that you will be prompted to reflect upon the values and beliefs you hold with respect to students, teaching, and educational practices generally, and consequently to reconsider actions which you take routinely and unconsciously in your everyday life as a teacher. Having reconsidered, you may then *choose* to do things differently.

What this book contains

The main part of the book comprises 20 case studies which have been selected to stimulate you to think about a wide array of problems that are faced by teachers. The people who wrote the case studies are ordinary teachers who actually faced the incidents which they describe as part of their everyday teaching experience. Their stories have the ring of truth about them and the cases have much relevance for teachers at differing levels and from differing subject areas. While in some instances there has been substantial editing, the case studies still retain much of their original form and substance.

Preceding each case is a brief paragraph identifying 'Issues Raised' and another containing 'Background' information. The former will allow you to distinguish at a glance the major issues which will be considered in a case, while the latter provides material which is not contained in the main parts of the case but which you may find helpful in understanding and interpreting the context of the case. Either in the case itself, or in the 'Background' section, you should thus find information on such things as the department and course concerned and the gender, age, background and experience of the teachers and students involved.

Each case study is in two or three parts and each part ends with a few questions. After the final part, there is a discussion of the case and a consideration of issues which have arisen. The discussion ends with a set of 'Questions for Personal Reflection', where you are invited to interpret for your own teaching practice any messages you may have picked up from the case. The case studies are arranged in no particular sequence, although we have attempted to put those which are likely to be more commonly encountered, or perhaps more straightforward, towards the front of the book. By skimming through the 'Issues Raised' paragraphs you may choose cases which you think may be interesting or relevant to your own situation. However, you will no doubt find that there are substantive issues of relevance for you in many of the cases, despite the fact that they describe subject areas or teaching methods different from your own.

A brief annotated bibliography and an appendix conclude the book. These have their origins in the seminar series we have ourselves run and from which the cases in this book were developed. The teachers who wrote the case studies attended these seminars, during which 'readings' were considered as well as cases. The readings were chosen to provoke thought and stimulate reflection. Some of these form the basis of the annotated bibliography, but it has been expanded to include some other resources which we think might be useful. However, the list is definitely *not* intended to be exhaustive or comprehensive and it is, in fact, a highly idiosyncratic selection from the large number of resources on teaching which are available.

The appendix describes how the cases in this book may be used for staff development seminars. The advice offered there is based on our own experience of running such seminar series over a number of years. This section of the book may therefore be of particular interest to people working through staff, professional or educational development units. If you are not such a person, you may still find this section worth reading before making contact with your own staff development people, or setting up your own sessions or discussion groups. We believe that the discussion of cases with colleagues is a valuable way in which the case studies may be utilized to help teachers learn about teaching.

The case studies

The cases we have selected reflect a wide range of issues, including personality clashes, challenges to authority, dealing with pranks in class, plagiarism, responding to an insult, assessment of student performance, evaluation of teacher performance, cultural differences, dealing with requests for preferential treatment by individual students, empathy for students, teachers' perceptions of their roles, and many others. At the same time, our impression is that several issues appear time after time. These include teacher-student relationships and the establishment of rapport between teachers and students, communication (between teachers and students but also between teachers and other teachers), and the establishment and maintenance of a teaching/learning contract. Although we have tried to highlight these issues whenever they appear, they are so prevalent that readers would be well advised to consider them to be of importance in every case study.

Each case study has at least two parts, and the break between parts occurs at a critical moment, where the teacher is left wondering: 'What do I do now?' At this point we invite you to step into the teacher's shoes and decide not only what you think *should* be done next but what you think *will actually happen* next given the circumstances of the case. After finding out what *did* happen, you will then be able to reflect on how the situation was handled and to consider some of the questions and issues raised by the case.

The cases thus tend to be somewhat climactic, with decision points where teachers must respond in what may be difficult or tense situations. We recognize that this does not necessarily reflect the day-to-day routine of teaching and learning, but we think the case structure and the subjects chosen encourage readers to *make* a decision, while at the same time promoting thought and reflection about what that decision might be. While the situations may not be typical in a 'day-to-day' sense, these *are* real problems which have arisen and which teachers have thought important enough to have presented as cases. We therefore believe that practices in the day-to-day world of teaching and learning can be informed by examining decisions taken in the somewhat climactic situations found in these cases.

Case discussions

At the end of each case study is a section of 'Discussion.' In this, we consider some of the major issues and questions which we think the case raises. The discussion is by no means exhaustive, nor do we suggest that these are the *only* important issues or questions which could be examined. You should therefore be neither disappointed nor surprised if you identify issues or perspectives which we have failed to mention. Similarly, you may strongly disagree with the interpretation we have offered. What we have attempted to do is to strike a balance between leaving each situation equivocal and open to individual interpretation on the one hand and tightly defining issues and providing guidance on the other. In the 'Discussion' section we have thus attempted to:

- identify and consider some of the key issues raised by the case study;
- identify what appear to be the interpretations placed on the situation by the various parties, and to suggest some alternative interpretations;
- consider some of the alternative courses of action open to the teacher in the case study and what the consequences of adopting those alternatives might be;
- comment on and raise questions about the decisions taken by the teacher in the case.

Again, you may feel that we have the balance wrong and have offered far too little guidance or alternatively far too much guidance, based on a total misinterpretation of the case! The best advice we can offer under these circumstances is that you try to discuss the case with other people, especially your colleagues. When you enter into such discussions you may be surprised at the variety of interpretations and judgements which are put forward, many of which will differ from your own.

Furthermore, it may appear that in some of our discussions we have been excessively critical of the teachers in several of the case studies. This has not been our intention. We recognize that in many instances they had to react under pressure and make immediate decisions. We, on the other hand, have had the advantages of time and hindsight to formulate our analyses. The purpose of our analysis is always to identify the variety of interpretations that can be placed upon the statements and actions of teachers who have been faced with important problems in their teaching practice.

We wish to emphasize that in the discussion we are not trying to give 'the right answer' to a problem. We do not believe that there is a simple and unequivocal 'right answer' in cases such as these. There may be some solutions which we would argue, under the circumstances, are better than others. The purpose of the discussion is, however, to explore what the circumstances appear to be to *each* of those involved, to identify *possible* ways of dealing with the problems, and to encourage you to make your own decisions based upon your reflections and interpretation of the case. The intent is that you may then use the insights gained from this experience to deal with, or to prevent, similar incidents which arise in your own teaching. Further, if the case studies heighten awareness of educational issues and of possible ways to deal with them, you may be better placed to anticipate and cope with new and unrelated problems.

How to use this book

We recommend that, in reading a case, you 'play the game' and read only Part One, before reflecting and noting your impressions of what is going on in the case, what course of action could be taken next, what you think *will* happen next, and what course of action *you* would pursue. The same applies to Part Two (or others where relevant). You will find questions at the end of each part of a case to assist you in framing your interpretation and response to what is happening. The questions tend to be appropriate for most cases, and include the following. At the end of Part One:

- what's going on here?
- how did this situation arise?
- how do the people involved in it see the situation?
- how might it be handled?
- what sorts of consequences might be expected from the possible actions?
- given the nature of the participants, how *will* it probably be dealt with?

After Part Two, the following additional questions could be considered:

- how well was the situation handled?
- what general issues are brought out by the case?

In addition to the questions that are appropriate for all cases, there may be others which are specific to the issues raised in an individual case. These are often referred to in the discussion of each case and in the final questions for personal reflection. After consideration of the case and its ramifications, readers are invited to consider two final questions each time:

- what do the case and its issues mean for me?
- do I need to consider changes to my teaching practices?

We think that as an individual reader you will derive valuable insights if you use the case studies and discussions in this way. However, we would again like to suggest that you could well find it valuable to meet with colleagues who are interested in teaching to share impressions of the cases and insights obtained from them. We have summarized in the appendix a method for such group discussion of the case studies in the form of a seminar series. However, a formal process such as a series of seminars is only one way in which the cases may be used, and you may gain valuable insights from informal discussion of the cases with your colleagues.

Whatever the format, consideration of the cases and issues by groups of colleagues has benefits beyond those which may be obtained from individual reading. First of all, in discussions with colleagues, teachers can confront their own perceptions and readings of cases and face the possibility, perhaps for the first time, that their own interpretations of teaching situations may not be shared by all. In justifying to colleagues their own interpretations of cases, they come face-to-face with their own philosophies of human nature and of education, and may thus become more reflective on their own practices. They are also forced to come to terms with the challenge posed by alternative conceptions and interpretations of each case. By having to understand each other's interpretations and the experiences and outlooks which shape them, teachers may be stimulated to re-examine and re-evaluate some of the central features of their own world views, or to consider and weigh more carefully what previously might have been rather hazy reasons for taking particular courses of action. The 'Discussion' sections in this book may give no more than a glimpse of the possibilities there are for quality discussion between colleagues on these issues.

Another major benefit of meeting with groups of colleagues to discuss issues in teaching is the support which such contact can provide. The case study *Goodies and Baddies* which appears in this book describes the lonely plight of a teacher seeking to improve teaching methods in an uncongenial environment. In this case the teacher is crushed by the first hint of failure, whereas we believe that the support of sympathetic colleagues could have resulted in a happier outcome.

Developing further as a teacher

From the discussion above, it is clear that we believe dialogue with colleagues concerning teaching should be commonplace. Teaching is supposedly such a central part of the higher education teacher's professional life that for this *not* to be the case would be worrying. We *are* worried. From our observations of teachers in higher education over many years, sustained and analytical discussion concerning what happens in the classroom is notable by its absence. Many teachers that we know comment on the fact that they seldom discuss teaching with their colleagues and rarely if ever meet teachers from other departments. Teachers tell us how they are frightened to describe or discuss openly what they do and what happens in their classrooms. Often they are afraid that they are doing things 'wrongly', that their lack of teaching expertise or knowledge will be exposed and they will be 'found out'. Loss of 'a collegial atmosphere' is possibly inevitable given the growth that has occurred in the numbers of staff, students and departments in large and complex modern universities, colleges and polytechnics. Perhaps 'collegiality' was little more than a myth in the past, anyway. But the coming together of practitioners to consider problems in teaching has been important to many teachers that we know and has provided a source of support and professional development which they had not previously experienced.

Apart from considering these cases on your own, or discussing them with colleagues, there are other avenues which you might care to explore. For example, there is much useful material in the wide array of books, journals and newspapers which pertain to education and teaching. We have referred to only a tiny proportion of these in the annotated bibliography at the back of the book. Another resource is the staff, professional or educational development unit which many institutions operate these days. Such a unit is likely to offer seminars, workshops, courses, consultations and resource collections on teaching. These, together with the advice and support which the staff of the unit can provide, may be extremely valuable to you as you seek to improve your understanding and practice of teaching.

Many resources are available, but deciding when and how to start is sometimes a problem. With the advent of formal review, appraisal and staff development systems within institutions, many teachers now find themselves having to produce 'aims and objectives' or 'plans' for the year ahead. There is therefore some scope for including in your plan for the coming year, research on and development of a particular area of your teaching. You may, for example, be exasperated by the unwillingness of students to talk in your tutorials, by their poor seminar presentations, by your own inability to finish a lecture on time, by the poor exam answers you receive following what you thought was your best lecturing ever etc. These and the vast number of other problems teachers encounter have been researched and there is good advice available on how to confront such problems. If you can choose and make headway on *one* problem this year, you may be taking the first step towards a richer and more satisfying career as a teacher. And if you can find a way to share your new knowledge and practice with your colleagues, and to listen to their problems and concerns, that satisfaction will be much further enriched. It may be that you can cooperate in considering how to improve a course or an aspect of teaching and to enter a process called 'action research' (there is more information on this in the annotated bibliography). The point is, of course, that while we have talked much about 'discussion' and 'reflection', for development to take place, these need eventually to find expression in *action*.

We hope that you enjoy reading the case studies, that you derive valuable insights from them, and that you find this book a useful step in your journey towards becoming a better teacher.

Reference

Martin, W B (ed.) (1981) *New Perspectives on Teaching and Learning*, New Directions for Teaching and Learning, no. 7, San Francisco, CA: Jossey-Bass.

Simon Cartwright and Paul Wilkinson

Case reporter: William Mackaness

Issues Raised

This case raises the question of how teachers make known their criteria for evaluating student assignments, especially with regard to the weighting of 'style' and 'content'. It also invites speculation on whether or when a teacher should admit to being wrong and how a teacher should relate to a 'difficult' student.

Background

In the course on Programming Principles which forms the basis of this case study, the classes are run as group discussions for 16 students at a time. The incident described occurred when the teacher was 28 years old and the students 20–22.

PART ONE

Simon Cartwright was a new lecturer in Information Systems; he had recently completed a PhD and had done some part-time teaching prior to his full-time employment. At the end of the first term, an essay was due from each of his 70 third year students. The assignment was entitled 'With reference to the principles of programming languages, compare and contrast the Turbo C programming language with an object-oriented programming language'.

A number of students found the topic tricky, so Simon gave them an extension to the beginning of the second term. He collected the essays and marked them, and was disappointed by the poor essay style that most students had demonstrated.

He did not publish marks and liked to hand essays back individually, thus giving an opportunity to discuss each essay in detail. This process was time-consuming because of frequent interruptions. At the end of one class, a group of students formed and requested the return of their essays. Simon saw this as a good opportunity to get rid of a batch of essays. One student sat down, the others grouped around, and Simon explained that the essay style was poor and that he had marked the essay down accordingly. The student (in a jocular fashion) complained that he had done 'tons of work' and was 'hard done by'. On second thoughts, Simon realized that the mark *was* harsh, but he did not want to appear 'weak' by significantly changing the mark. The student grumbled something about 'content, not style' and Simon agreed to re-assess the essay. With that said, the student changed seats with Paul Wilkinson.

Paul Wilkinson was a sullen student who consistently arrived eight minutes late for every lecture and appeared almost to deride other students in the lecture group. Simon sensed that Paul enjoyed being an 'alternative voice' who was proud of the fact that he already had a degree in philosophy.

Simon pulled Paul's essay from the pile. In contrast to the previous essay, Simon had given Paul's a high mark. Simon made comments that reflected the mark and stated that the essay, though not entirely relevant, was written in a good style, appeared to take a philosophical stance, was entertaining to read and was 'imaginative'. This contrasted with other students' essays; while their content appeared relevant, it was not obvious that some students fully understood what they were writing.

The student then leaned back in his chair and announced to the assembled group that he had done absolutely no work for the essay, knew nothing of the programming languages, and had made the whole essay up. He went on to say that although the previous student had done far more work than he had, Simon had given a much lower mark, and that 'no other student would get away with it on any other course'!

- *What do you think Simon did next?*
- *What would you have done at this point?*

PART TWO

Simon thought that perhaps he had not spent as much time on marking the essays as he should have. However, he did not reduce the mark on Paul's essay. He argued that the mark reflected an ability to communicate ideas. Using time as an excuse, he then called a halt to the proceedings.

Simon had been keen to show that he was receptive to 'alternative answers'. He also wanted to encourage Paul to participate in a more productive manner in both tutorials and lectures. Given these considerations and the fact that Paul's essay had been one of the more readable ones, Simon had marked it generously.

He next discussed the situation with several friends and talked to other lecturers about the student. They painted a picture of an unresponsive student who had failed quite a few components of the course. Some suggested that Simon might have challenged him by asking him to explain what he meant by some of the sentences, thereby showing that he *had* in fact done some work.

Simon resolved never again to hand back essays in group situations, and he was annoyed with himself for having so 'misread' the student. He stopped making attempts to involve Paul and proceeded with care whenever their paths crossed. The student went on to complete other items of work, on which he performed poorly. Simon set another essay and although he was careful to mark fairly, he marked Paul's essay down for containing trivia!

- *How well do you think Simon handled this incident?*
- *If faced with a similar incident, how would you have acted; what would you have done differently?*

Discussion

In this, as in some of the other cases which follow in this book, one is struck by the openness with which the case is reported. During the exchange the teacher realizes that he has made more than one mistake, but he is not quite sure what he could have done differently. How often as teachers have we been in a similar position?

Perhaps the first question that can be raised has to do with the expectations of the teacher and students concerning what was required from the essay assignment. It seems that this was never discussed nor made explicit, thus explaining the distance which appears to separate the teacher and students when the marks are discussed. Having said this, however, it must be recognized that no matter how much discussion precedes an open-ended activity such as this form of essay writing, the mark awarded will always be open to challenge because of the possibility of differing interpretive positions being taken by students and teachers. The question is whether the range of interpretation could usefully be restricted by discussion taking place between teacher and students concerning what they see as being the major objectives of the assignment and the criteria by which it will be evaluated.

The major issue of contention concerns the relative 'weighting' placed on 'content' and 'style'. It seems that many students (including the one to whom Simon first speaks) have included reasonable 'content' but have not argued or presented the content in a particularly enlightening or interesting way. On the other hand, Paul Wilkinson's essay stands out as being well written and interesting, even though it may be short on 'content'. It is easy to see how the respective positions of teacher and student bring this about. The students want to show that they 'know' the material by reproducing what they consider to be the 'core' of this. The teacher, faced with essay after essay containing the same information, is naturally drawn to something different, something innovative or with a 'spark' which distinguishes it from the rest.

Simon realizes that he may have been too hard on the first essay and overly impressed with the 'style' of the second. But what can he do about it now? He does not have the luxury of being able to change his mind in the privacy of his own office. Even if he had been in his own office, would it be fair to change the grade on one essay without reconsidering the others? The fact is that the 'action' is taking place in front of a number of very interested (if not aggrieved) students. Given the circumstances, it is perhaps surprising that Simon agrees to review the grade of the first student at all.

The confrontation with Paul Wilkinson is more serious and threatening. It calls into question not only Simon's professionalism (by suggesting he had not taken the time to mark carefully), but also his competence (by suggesting that he cannot distinguish between an essay written by someone who knew something about the subject and someone who did not). While Simon appears to admit the former to himself, should he admit it to the students? Would he lose further credibility by offering to look at his marking on this essay, too, or would he gain respect from the students by admitting fallibility? The answer to this may well depend upon the reader's conception of what constitutes a 'proper' relationship between teacher and student. As to the latter point concerning Simon's competence, could or should he try to demonstrate that Paul really *did* know something about the subject? Some research within higher education suggests that there is no such thing as a good generic 'writing style' or the ability to write a 'good essay' irrespective of content and understanding. Would it be worthwhile for Simon to pursue this line by trying to demonstrate Paul's under-standing, albeit that this could well be at a level somewhat different from that of the other students? If he chose to do this, Simon has the essay itself to which he could refer. He also has Paul, the student, although trying to coax knowledge and understanding out of a student who is determined to show that he has neither, could be problematic to say the least.

Finally, there is the point about the nature of the relationship between Simon and Paul. Not only has Paul raised the issue but he has done so in front of others and in such a way as to cause a maximum of embarrassment for Simon. It is clear that Simon is upset with Paul, irrespective of the particular issue in question. Whereas Simon had previously tried to engage and include Paul in classes, after this incident he feels somewhat betrayed; he stops making efforts to involve the student and is very wary of him in future encounters. While this is a completely understandable position to take, it is perhaps worth considering whether alternative courses of action were open to Simon which would have confronted the problem of their relationship. In other words, should Simon have continued in his attempts to involve Paul after the incident had occurred, could he have tried to get nearer to Paul rather than to have withdrawn?

From Simon's standpoint following this incident, that would appear to be a difficult thing for him to attempt. On the other hand, it seems obvious that Paul is disenchanted with not only Simon, but other aspects of the course too. If Simon could forget his own sense of betrayal and injury, there might at least be a chance that if he tried with Paul again, he (or one of his colleagues) might be able to shed light on the nature of Paul's problems. As matters stand, there appears little prospect for a happier resolution of Paul's antipathy towards all concerned with the course.

QUESTIONS FOR PERSONAL REFLECTION

- *Do you explicitly discuss the objectives of your assignments and the criteria by which they will be evaluated? How far are students asked to participate in this process?*
- *What is your position on the 'content' versus 'style' argument? Do you make your own position clear to students?*
- *How do you react when the case is made or you see for yourself that you have made a mistake (eg, in grading)? What course of action would you tend to take and why?*
- *How do you act towards 'sullen' or disruptive students? What position would you take with respect to a student who has sought to undermine and challenge you?*
- *Are there any other implications or lessons to be drawn from this case which have application in your own teaching? Is there anything in your own teaching practice that you need to reconsider after having read and reflected on this case?*

Just Desserts

Case reporter: Gordon Sanderson

Issues Raised

This case raises the issue of how teachers and students interact when they move outside of the normal classroom setting. Focused upon a dramatic incident, it invites readers to reflect upon how they would handle a difficult out-of-class situation.

Background

The medical student class dinner that is the focus of the case took place in the mid-1980s in the middle of the last term of the year. As usual, it was held in a large room in the Student Union. The male teacher was from a clinical department and had been teaching the same course for 14 years. He was 39 years old at the time, while the students were mostly 20 or 21.

PART ONE

Invitations to student functions come through the internal mail fairly frequently. Most of them are *pro forma* invitations, but occasionally one is invited personally, or so it is made to appear. This class dinner for medical students was one such occasion. The invitation was delivered by a student whom I had got to know reasonably well. Although this was not the first time that I had accepted, I normally don't accept such invitations. However, I felt that as I had got to know more than a handful of the students in this particular year, I would be happy to go along this time.

The theme of the dinner was a 'tropical evening'. I decided that, since it was mid-winter and my suntan had faded, I would just wear a lounge suit. This was by no means out of keeping, as the staff who attend these functions normally do not wear fancy dress.

The dinner was well attended, as they usually are. Most of the class of 150 or so were present and about six members of staff were there as well. The meal was a buffet and the food was taken in a reasonably orderly fashion. Having enjoyed the main course and a glass or two of wine, I was fairly relaxed by the time dessert was being consumed. I decided that because my suit was already a fairly tight fit, I wouldn't actually have any dessert but would make do with a cup of coffee. During the dessert, one of the students who had been going from table to table with his camera asked if he could take my photograph. I had no particular objections to this and so I agreed. I became aware that there was an inordinate delay as the camera was being focused and various other adjustments were being made. Then from behind me a hand appeared holding a plate of pavlova (meringue pie) and whipped cream and this was duly pushed into my face. At that moment the flash of the camera went off and from all around me there were howls of mirth, which quickly spread to the entire room.

- *What do you think the person did next?*
- *What would you have done in this situation?*

PART TWO

My initial reaction was reflex: I tried to wipe the cream and pavlova off my face in order to see who had perpetrated the crime. However, by then he or she had disappeared into the crowd. I wiped the remainder of the mess off as best I could using a handkerchief and napkins. At this stage one of the kitchen staff took pity on me and led me through into the kitchen area, where she tried to sponge the cream from my suit. I then crept back to my seat as inconspicuously as I could. Fortunately, the hilarity had died away by then.

In their defence, the students at the table where I was sitting were remorseful and apologetic although they steadfastly refused to give me the name of the person who had actually done the deed! I was then approached by the Associate Dean for Student Affairs, who was also present. He suggested that these dinners had been getting out of hand recently and that this unruly behaviour had been discouraging members of staff from attending. He recommended that I make a formal complaint in order to try to prevent this sort of thing occurring again in the future.

I was by now feeling both humiliated and damp and it wasn't long before I found an excuse to take my leave and head for home. Just as I was leaving, the social representative of the class approached me, apologized on behalf of the class and suggested that I send the bill for the cost of dry-cleaning my suit to the student executive.

- *What do you think the person did next after he had time to reflect upon the incident?*
- *What course of action should he have taken?*
- *What would you have done after the incident?*

PART THREE

I decided not to lodge a formal complaint and not even to forward my dry-cleaning bill to the students.

A few days later the social representative came to see me, again apologized on behalf of the students and explained to me that the person concerned was very remorseful. I suggested that his or her apology wouldn't go amiss, but this was not ultimately forthcoming.

However, I was approached during the next term by a couple of members of the student executive, who said that they thought that I had handled the affair very well and they asked whether I would consider being the vice-patron of the student executive for the following year. That was an invitation which I accepted readily.

- *How well do you think the person handled the incident? What other options were available and what might have been the consequences of taking them?*
- *How would you have handled the incident? Would you have done things differently?*

Discussion

In a classroom, the roles and behaviours of teacher and student are bounded by convention. Expectations of what is acceptable, of what can and should happen are for the most part taken for granted. The teacher inherits a tradition of expectation that he or she will exercise control and have power over the situation. Once one steps outside of this 'normal range', the teacher-student relationship falls open to a greater degree of uncertainty and negotiation. This is accentuated as students assume a more powerful and controlling role in social situations. This case study raises the difficult issue of relationships between teachers and students outside of class, especially social occasions on student 'territory'. It is also highly likely that whatever happens between teachers and students outside of the classroom will affect the nature of the relationship within the classroom.

There is scope within this case for readers to adopt any of a variety of views. This can range from considering what happened to be a mild joke to be laughed off, to considering it both insulting and an assault, to be dealt with very severely. Whether one considers it a joke or an insult will obviously influence the answer to the question: How should the teacher respond? In fact there is room for either interpretation and it is possible to marshal evidence for each from the case notes. There are tantalizing hints about the personality of the teacher and the relationship between teacher and students. Many questions may thus suggest themselves, some of which could be as follows.

Would the same thing have happened if the teacher had dressed to suit the theme? Would the students have wanted to do the same thing if they had asked for and received permission first? What sorts of factors influence the susceptibility of individuals to such 'pranks'? Should a fuss be made or should the whole episode be played down? Although the incident was clearly outside the classroom, would its significance and consequences necessarily be divorced from the relationship between teacher and students within class? Is it possible for a teacher offended in such a way to obtain satisfaction without at the same time alienating the students? If so, how?

There is insufficient information in the case to be certain about what is going on, or about the background to the incident and the intentions of the students involved. Most people who have considered this case think that the teacher involved did what was appropriate when the incident occurred: he did not make a great fuss and retired with as much dignity as he could muster. Alternatively, some people have said they would have stopped proceedings and delivered a rebuke, others that they would have stormed right out of the room, and yet others how they may well have joined in the 'slapstick'.

Similarly, in what happens after, there is often some debate about an appropriate course of action. Some would say the incident should be laughed off and forgotten, others would register their displeasure without taking any formal measures, while others again would seek to institute disciplinary proceedings. The teacher in the case decided to let the incident pass, although he did expect an apology from the student concerned. When this did not eventuate, he did not pursue the matter further. It is perhaps disappointing that the student who was mainly responsible did not feel secure enough in his or her relationship with the teacher to make an apology. Perhaps this is indicative of an undeveloped relationship between the teacher and students, as had they known each other better, the incident might never have happened. As it was, however, the course of action taken by the teacher appears to have been vindicated and the students, grateful for the forbearance he displayed, indicated their thanks by inviting him to be vice-patron of the student executive. If you had been in the teacher's position, and had taken different actions, you might find it interesting to try and foresee the consequences of those actions, and whether the end result would have been better or worse.

As you consider what action you would have taken, you may also be able to draw parallels with less extreme situations you have experienced yourself while meeting students outside of the classroom. As you consider your relationship with students in such circumstances, you may wish to think about your own comfort, expectations and behaviours in these contexts. This may give you some insight as to how you wish to act in your dealings with students outside of the classroom, whether you wish to initiate outside contacts with students and whether such experiences can be used to good effect within the classroom.

Our own experience has been that encountering students in non-formal situations helps to broaden and deepen our relationships with students. While such situations are problematic, the hard work involved in establishing new perspectives in relationships with students can pay dividends in terms of the trust, rapport and mutual understandings subsequently made possible in the classroom.

QUESTIONS FOR PERSONAL REFLECTION

- *How do you presently encounter students outside of the normal classroom situation? Would you like to have more or less such contact? Why?*

- *Are some non-formal contacts with students more problematic for you than others? If so, what kind of situation is more problematic and why is this so?*
- *How do you tend to act when meeting students on non-formal occasions? How do you think students view you on such occasions? Could your behaviour be misconstrued by students; would you wish to change it in any way?*
- *Are there any other implications or lessons to be taken from this case which have ramifications for your relationships with students? Is there anything in your relationship with students or your teaching practice which you need to reconsider after having read and reflected on this case?*

Did She or Did She Not?

Case reporter: Giora Shapira

Issues Raised

Plagiarism is the issue raised in this case. A talented, advanced student submits what appears to be a plagiarized paper. The teacher has to weigh up the circumstances surrounding the case and has to decide on an appropriate course of action.

Background

The Advanced Contract course is offered to third or fourth year students in the law faculty of a university in New Zealand. When this incident occurred, the teacher was 48 years old and had a total of 12 years of teaching experience. The student was 21.

PART ONE

Peter had been a Senior Lecturer in Law for six years when he first took the Advanced Contract, LLB Honours course in 1985. There were eight students in the class. It was to be run by way of weekly seminars, with each student writing and presenting two papers during the year. Peter offered the students a list of possible topics for the papers, but they were free, and indeed encouraged, to choose their own topics subject to Peter's approval. To give the students time to look for topics and to write the papers, Peter decided that the seminars would start several weeks into the first term of the teaching year.

Two weeks into term, Dinah, a student in the course, came to see Peter. She said she wanted to write a paper on *Cheques in Accord and Satisfaction* – a topic not on Peter's list. Briefly, this involves a situation where A owes money to B for, say, the purchase of goods, or for services rendered. B claims the money. A admits the debt, but only a certain part of it. A sends a letter to B saying something like, 'I dispute the figure of $1000 claimed by you. According to our agreement I owe you only $600. I enclose a cheque for $600 in full payment of your claim.' B banks the cheque and sues for the rest. What is the legal position? Should the banking of the cheque be interpreted as an acceptance by B of A's position and an undertaking to waive the rest? In other words, if B insists on the full sum, does he have to *send back* the cheque and sue for the $1000? The leading New Zealand case is a 1978 High Court decision called *Lifeguard Industries*. The court held that in the absence of contrary agreement the party who banks the cheque accepts it in full 'accord and satisfaction' of the claim and waives any further claim.

Peter asked Dinah what made her choose the topic. She said that she had always found the *Lifeguard* case interesting. She disagreed with the Court's decision and preferred the American position, which had gone the other way. Peter approved the topic. After Dinah left his office, Peter could not help thinking how impressive she was. She was precise and got quickly to the core of a problem. She had an air of detachment about her but at the same time seemed well in control. Peter had not taught her before, but from colleagues he learned that Dinah appeared to be a brilliant student. She did not volunteer much, but when she spoke others listened. She was confident and ambitious and was obviously destined for great things. Her father was a well known lawyer, a senior partner in a large practice. Peter looked forward to reading Dinah's paper on *Accord and Satisfaction*.

When she handed in her draft, three weeks later, he was not disappointed. She scored highly on analytical framework, research and style. In her conclusions she criticized the *Lifeguard* position and put forward a well reasoned argument in favour of the opposite, American position. Peter enjoyed the paper and reflected on how rare it was for a law student to submit a straight A quality paper. He made a few comments on the draft and approved the paper for presentation, subject to his comments. The paper was to be graded after the presentation, on both the written work and the oral presentation.

A week before the seminar in which Dinah was to present her paper, copies of the paper were handed out to the other members of the class. Tony, a young colleague of Peter, received a copy, too. Tony was a teacher of the Law of Contract and sat in on the Advanced Contract seminars out of interest.

Dinah's presentation was as succinct as her writing. There followed a lively discussion, in which she ably defended her position. This was the first seminar of the year and Peter was delighted it had set such a high standard. He was about to dismiss the class when Tony asked if he could have a word in private. They withdrew to another room, and Tony came straight to the point: 'I am sorry to tell you this, Peter, but Dinah has copied large parts of her paper from published work'.

Tony produced from his pocket a copy of the case note in which Duncan discussed the *Lifeguard* case. Duncan was a veteran law lecturer at a nearby university and his note on *Lifeguard* had been published in a local law journal in 1978. A quick look was sufficient to convince Peter that Dinah had indeed plagiarized whole passages from Duncan's work.

- *What do you think Peter should do when he returns to the classroom?*
- *What diverse courses of action are open to him?*
- *What do you think Peter actually did next?*

PART TWO

Peter was flabbergasted, his previous enthusiasm for the paper turning into bitter disappointment. His first reaction was to storm back to the classroom, give Dinah a fierce dressing-down, and fail her on the paper. But he soon got hold of himself, realizing that he needed some time to think it over. He asked Tony 'not to breathe a word about it to anyone'. They returned to the class. Peter thanked Dinah and the class and dismissed the class, asking Dinah to come back the following Wednesday to collect her marked paper.

During the following weekend Peter could hardly stop thinking about the incident. Why did she do it? How could she do it? Peter spent a number of hours comparing Dinah's paper with Duncan's. He had been aware of Duncan's work but did not remember it well enough to notice the similarities immediately. Dinah's was a 15,000 word paper, while Duncan's was much shorter. In four different places Dinah had incorporated whole passages of Duncan's work, verbatim, into her own text without mention of it.

As Peter continued to compare the two papers, his puzzlement grew. First, the lifting from Duncan was restricted to the first few pages of Dinah's work, which were mainly background. The main thrust came later and turned on matters and ideas not discussed by Duncan at all. All this later material was original, as far as Peter could tell, and this time he checked it very carefully. Dinah's paper was much superior to Duncan's. Second, it is very common in legal writing to refer to, and cite, published work, which the writer can use as building blocks for his or her own work. All Dinah had to do was to acknowledge her source and she would have been in the clear, the quality of her paper intact. Again, it is not uncommon for a law student to use an idea or a re-worded phrase from a published work without attribution – the temptation is strong. But plagiarism on such a scale – whole passages word for word? How could she hope to get away with it? (Even if Peter did not notice, someone else would.) Was there an innocent explanation for Dinah's behaviour? It was such a foolish and reckless thing for her to do. At the same time it was plagiarism, as clear as the nose on your face, and, surely, everyone knew what plagiarism was.

Peter considered his options. He could have passed the matter on to the dean, as a disciplinary matter. But this would have been passing the buck. The dean would have no choice but to throw the book at her. Peter knew that he had to deal with the matter himself. Whatever his decision, he would have to take account of his own strong feelings about cheating, the effect on Dinah's career, and the effect on other students' morale.

He was still strongly inclined to give her a piece of his mind and fail her on the paper. He knew this would be devastating – she would have to withdraw from the course, and perhaps from the Honours programme. For a high-flier like her it would be a crash landing. And the talk around the law school. . . .

Peter decided to confront Dinah with the evidence. He wanted to surprise her and watch her reaction. He still secretly hoped that she could convince him that there had been some mistake. When she eventually came, she pre-empted him. 'I hear you are unhappy about my use of Duncan's work' were her opening words. (Tony must have talked.) 'Unhappy?', bellowed Peter. 'This is cheating!' Dinah, obviously distressed but still in control, proceeded to argue that her paper was much different from Duncan's. She dealt with many things that he hadn't and her conclusions were different. She hinted that her paper was superior. She produced her paper and Duncan's and pointed out how different they were.

Finally, she came up with a relevant explanation. She found Duncan's work useful in the parts that set out the practical background and those that merely summarized (without analysis) the *Lifeguard* decision. 'I did not think I could improve on it. He had done it, it was merely descriptive, so I used it'. To Peter's question why she did not make a mention of it, she answered that it was the first paper of that nature she had written; she thought the emphasis was on ideas and analysis and did not realize it was necessary to quote.

When she left, Peter was still dismayed. He was better informed but none the wiser. Again, he was impressed with the force of Dinah's argument, if not with its merits. He continued to agonize over the decision which he promised to give Dinah in a few days.

- *What do you think Peter's final decision will be?*
- *Having had a chance to hear the student's explanation, have you changed your mind about what should be done?*

PART THREE

Peter could not let cheating go unpunished. If Dinah had cheated, she had to be punished severely. That meant marking the paper as nil. Anything less would give Dinah and the other students the wrong message. On the other hand, Peter was only too aware of the effect of such an action on Dinah's future. She would fail the course (the final grade was made up of the two seminar papers) and perhaps the entire Honours programme. And it would be a large blot on her record.

If there could be any doubt as to her intent, she should be given the benefit of that doubt. Could it be that she had acted stupidly, rather than maliciously? Peter did not buy her explanation, but it did raise some doubt. It also provided an explanation to the question uppermost in Peter's mind: Why did she do it?

Peter decided he had to give Dinah the benefit of the doubt. Still, she had to be punished, though not as severely as she would have been for cheating. The punishment had to serve as a stern warning.

At first Peter thought about marking the paper down drastically, to something like C or C+, but on second thoughts he decided against it. Even discounted for Duncan, it was a first-class paper and to mark it as C would just not be right. Besides, a C on an Honours paper like this was tantamount to a failure and was likely to affect her final class of Honours. Peter had to remind himself that Dinah's intent was the crucial element and that he had given her the benefit of the doubt on that. Peter decided to reduce Dinah's mark by two grades (from A to B+) and give Dinah a stern warning.

Before handing back the paper he consulted with two junior colleagues. They had both themselves been students not that long before and could give Peter perspectives of both teachers and students. One was Tony, a fairly up and down fellow. The other was Vicky, a newly appointed assistant lecturer. She was a stickler for authority – she once refused to mark a bi-weekly assignment because it was handed in 15 minutes late! Peter talked to Tony and Vicky separately, giving them his reasons. Somewhat to his surprise, they both agreed with his conclusions.

Peter wrote on Dinah's paper: 'Using other people's work without attribution is cheating. It will not be tolerated. I am giving you the benefit of the doubt, hoping it will be a lesson you will not forget. Your mark is B+, reduced from A, for plagiarism'. He handed the paper back to Dinah, repeating his written comment. She sat expressionless, thanked him curtly, and left without another word.

Dinah eventually completed the course with an A-, having obtained a straight A in her second paper. Communication between Peter and Dinah remained cordial, neither ever mentioning the incident again.

Dinah graduated the next year with first class Honours. She later joined a leading law firm and is known as bright and hard working. She is rapidly making a name for herself.

- How do you feel about the way in which Peter responded to this incident?
- Would you have acted differently if you had been faced with the same situation? If so, why and in what way?

Discussion

The issue in this case is clearly the problem of plagiarism and how to deal with it. In much of its tone and in the teacher's initial reaction to the discovery, we see reflected an abhorrence that many teachers have of this form of 'cheating' and the inclination to punish it severely. In fact, many teachers would probably chastise Peter for being so indecisive and for imposing too mild a penalty. However, it is to his credit that Peter considered all sides of the issue before deciding upon his action.

From the case, we gather that Peter shares the strong feelings of many teachers about plagiarism and that under appropriate circumstances he would be willing to respond harshly. Unlike many others, however, he is willing to weigh the evidence about what might have been the student's *intent* before responding. In this regard, it may be relevant that the teacher was a lawyer, teaching in a faculty of law. In fact, from his case report we can see quite clearly that he tried to see the student's side, even though in the final analysis he could not be certain of her reasons. He tried to imagine why she would even *think* of doing what she did if she was aware of the nature and consequences of plagiarism. The material which she used was only for background and it represented only a small portion of her own work, which went well beyond the plagiarized material. If she really had been aware of the problem of plagiarism, what earthly reason could she have had for jeopardizing the whole of her own work merely by failing to attribute a small portion of what she used as background? Considerations like these would tend to support the contention that the student had really only committed an honest mistake through lack of understanding of what was involved. What is more, had she been an average student at an early stage of her education, such arguments would probably have been sufficient to allow the teacher to reach a conclusion.

Dinah, however, is recognized as a brilliant student and she is taking an advanced course. Peter considers that she would surely be aware of what constitutes plagiarism and how strongly teachers feel about it. In Peter's discussion with Dinah we find a rather bland indication that perhaps the student was not aware of the rules, but the teacher obviously finds this hard to believe. Although there is no way of knowing, one could also question how much Peter's reaction was influenced by his acknowledgement of her impressiveness, his initial markedly positive reaction to her paper, and his own failure to spot the plagiarism, which was brought to his attention by a junior colleague. As in most such cases, Peter was left unsure of whether the student was fully aware of what she had done and why she had done it. This being the case, he decided that, while doubt remained, she was entitled to the benefit of that doubt.

He further tempered his ultimate decision by considering his options and their potential effects on Dinah's career and on the morale of the other students in the class. Interestingly, although he agonized over them, many of the issues and options were not touched upon in his report of the case. Despite the fact that he was concerned about the others in the class, there is no indication that his reaction to Dinah's plagiarism was conveyed formally to the rest of the class nor that he took the obvious step of ensuring that written guidelines about the nature and consequences of plagiarism were distributed to students entering the course.

Did Peter really consider all of his options? He appears to have considered only the extent to which he should downgrade the paper, as if assuming that the whole document was uniformly tainted. Yet he also acknowledged that much of the paper added substantially and indepen- dently to Duncan's previous work. This being the case, the plagiarized segments might have been excluded and the rest of the paper marked on its own (with or without a penalty deducted for the plagiarism). Alternatively, if Peter accepted that Dinah's intent was uncertain, perhaps she could have been given an opportunity to submit another paper. At the most liberal extreme, because it was such a good paper independent of the plagiarized portions, the small amount of plagiarism might have been ignored in the grading but the student and the class made aware of the rules about plagiarism for the future.

Perhaps the most frustrating things about cases of plagiarism are that teachers outline what is *bad* practice only *after* the event, and the event is often associated with a major or final project. If teachers could show what is *good* practice *before* students take on an assignment, and if they would instil this at levels lower than that of a final project, it might well be that many potential cases of plagiarism could be nipped in the bud.

QUESTIONS FOR PERSONAL REFLECTION

- *What steps do you take to minimize the chances of plagiarism occurring?*
- *When faced with what appears to be a flagrant act of plagiarism, how would you respond?*
- *How do you deal with instances of 'plagiarism' which are more equivocal? Do you have a 'stock' response or do you take account of considerations such as:*
  - *uncertainty about the student's knowledge of the rules;*
  - *uncertainty about the student's intent;*
  - *the significance of the plagiarized portions of the student's work;*
  - *possible repercussions of the response for the student and for others in the class;*
  - *the desire to penalize cheating and to deter others?*
- *Does this case have any other implications for your own teaching practice?*

Too Much 'Glasnost' in the Classroom?

Case reporter: Colin Dowsett

Issues Raised

The main issues raised by this case study are classroom communication, rapport between teachers and students, and the consequences of a mismatch between the perceptions of teachers and students about the teaching/learning contract.

Background

The incidents described occurred during 1989. The male teacher was 40 years old at the time, while the students were about 20. It was the teacher's second year of teaching the course and his teaching experience overall was three years.

PART ONE

The course

This incident occurred when I was teaching the first term of a third-year course in Russian translation. In this course, the students were required to translate passages from Russian into English. This was not their first 'hands-on' experience of translation as they began making translations in the second year.

The course was completely internally assessed. The students' assignment load was one translation every week. However, they could choose out of their marked work the best 14 out of 18 translations completed over the course of the year, and only these were taken into account for the final mark. Moreover, although work was assigned every week, I allowed the students two weeks in which to translate and hand in the assigned passage. They were free to consult any aids they wished, including dictionaries and grammars.

The class composition

The class comprised seven students, two of whom were taking honours in

Russian. All were women, and they were a closely-knit group. In addition, there was an auditor from another university, a male student. He was attending the course for interest only and was not required to submit work. However, he did so and it was corrected.

The situation

As per normal, I began this particular class by handing back the homework which I had marked and which I was now prepared to discuss with the students. I had set them an extract from a speech by Mikhail Gorbachev to Ukrainian workers. The students had clearly found this difficult and had done poorly, as was reflected by the marks awarded. However, I felt that the performance on this occasion had less to do with the degree of difficulty of the passage than with the students' lack of concerted effort.

Before actually describing what happened, I should say something about my marking system and about why I chose the Gorbachev speech for translation. Bearing in mind the different problems associated with translation, I cultivated what I thought was a fair system of marking. One mark was deducted where the original Russian had clearly been misunderstood. Half a mark was deducted where the student had apparently understood the meaning but had rendered it poorly into English. I gave bonus marks (added one mark back on) where I thought that the translation had been exceptionally well done at particular points.

As to the Gorbachev speech, I must confess that this was hardly gripping stuff and was, in its way, difficult. Like most political speeches, Gorbachev's was very prolix, using long sentence structures with multiple subordinate clauses. At the same time, I felt that this offered the students an insight into the possibilities of the Russian language. This was also good contemporary standard Russian. In addition, the majority of these students had declared themselves to be uninterested in literature, so I thought that I should try to choose passages of a non-literary nature. My main concern was that they have exposure to as many different styles of Russian as possible.

What happened

After handing back their homework, I began to point out their errors and noted that they were translating, in some places, too freely. As I was speaking I could sense in the class a mood which manifested itself as a vague mumbling. The first challenge came from the auditor, who, in an aggressive manner, asked: 'So, faced with Russian you can't put into English, what do you do? Isn't it better to translate freely?' I replied that it was necessary to be sure that there weren't any satisfactory ways of translating parts of passages with the greatest accuracy. In my opinion, such instances were rare. Translations should not be marred by paraphrase.

Then came another broadside from one of the other students, who said: 'You give us passages out of the middle of things. We don't know what the passage is dealing with'. At this point, the others chimed in with their agreement. I replied that all extracts for translation are of necessity taken out of larger texts but that the section I had taken from the Gorbachev speech was, I felt, self-contained enough to be comprehensible and, certainly, could be translated.

Another student asked, 'Can't you give us children's literature to translate?' I was taken aback by this and somewhat exasperated. I replied that, yes, I could but that all they would end up being able to read was children's literature.

The atmosphere was getting hot now and was ripe for a crisis. This wasn't long in coming!

The crisis

Going over the Gorbachev speech, I noted that, because it was political rhetoric and Gorbachev was using an impersonal manner of address in Russian, the pronoun 'one' should be used in translation. This was appropriate here, I said, even if somewhat stilted in everyday speech.

The auditor then said: 'That's awful! You said yourself that it's stilted. Nobody should use that. We were taught in school not to!' The class was solidly behind him, although a few remained silent. I stood by my choice and heard someone, under her breath, mutter an unkind remark. I knew the students were unhappy, but I knew, too, that this particular outburst was only a symptom of their general discontent. But I was angry with them – and I think it showed. It was really going to be difficult to get them back on an even keel. What had happened? How could I save the situation?

- *What would you advise the teacher to do next?*
- *Based on your interpretation of the situation, what do you think actually happened?*

PART TWO

To regain equilibrium, I suggested that they translate the 'unseen' exercise which we never got to tackle in class, as an alternative assignment. This was at a much easier level and gave them the chance to get a better mark. This appeared to placate them, but I didn't feel very good about it. I thought I had retreated.

Next class, I arrived and continued as if nothing had happened. In the interim period, although I had not quite purchased the pharmacy's whole supply of antacid tablets, I did worry about how to continue. The incident had raised many questions for me:

Was I to blame for what happened?
Was this merely group 'chemistry'?
What role did the auditor play in all this? Did he act as a catalyst or was his 'contribution' more than that? Did he feel he had to play a 'male role' in an all-female class? (After this incident, interestingly, he no longer came to the class.)

I finally decided to give them slightly easier passages without lowering what I considered to be the essential standard to which the students should aspire. I did understand that, for them, the marks meant everything, but I saw the purpose of the course and my role in it primarily as getting them to a level of proficiency which would enable them to pick up any sort of Russian text and read it. They did fairly well until the end of the term but not spectacularly. Some failed to hand in several weeks' work!

By prior arrangement at the beginning of the year, a colleague took over the class for the rest of the course. She did not appear to have any major problems with them but she did feel that their approach to the work was distinctly sluggish.

- *How well did the teacher handle the situation?*
- *What might he have done differently and what might have been the outcome?*
- *Would you have done anything differently?*

Discussion

Several of the case studies in this book highlight issues of the teaching/ learning contract, communication and rapport between teachers and students. This may be interpreted as one of these cases. Through the eyes of the teacher, however, the problem appears to be mainly one of dealing with a cantankerous group of students who fail to apply themselves sufficiently to a moderately difficult task, and then complain when their work is criticized. Although the teacher questions his own role in the incident, we are left in little doubt that, to him, most of the blame rests with the students. While we can see his version of events, we must also try to put ourselves into the students' shoes and ask different questions from those which the teacher asked himself. It is suggested that other teachers who find themselves in similar situations may care to do likewise, and so realize that they and their students could well have different questions concerning a course, or give different answers to the same questions. Recognition of this may lead to a repertoire of approaches for dealing with situations, or even to the prevention or minimization of the impact of such situations by anticipation and early intervention.

The first item of note is the one-sidedness of the teaching/learning contract, at least as it is described in the case study. We can see the *teacher's* impression of what the contract is and what he believes the students should get out of the course, but what were the *students'* impressions? Especially for a small, advanced course, it should have been easy for the teacher to consult or negotiate with the students to design a course which met their expectations as well as his own. There are, of course, the counter-arguments that the teacher knows best what the students should get from the course and that he has to maintain standards. While such points may be borne in mind, the conflict which is apparent in the case study suggests that the teacher never adequately *explained* his perceptions of course goals to the students. Even if such communication was not intended to be followed by negotiation, it might at least have clarified matters for the students so that they knew exactly what to expect.

Part of the teacher's aim for the course, for example, is obviously to help students to distinguish translation strategies appropriate to particular circumstances and texts. Much of this has to do with the *purpose* of the translation. Did he ever discuss this with the students and did they discuss together the strategy they might adopt for a particular text? Had they done so, the students may have better appreciated why free translation in order to aid their own understanding was but one option, serving a particular circumstance and purpose. From the teacher's point of view, a stricter translation without paraphrasing was more appropriate, presumably for the purposes of accuracy and capturing the tone of the text, which he thought to be of major importance. Had the students been aware of the teacher's thinking on these matters, then when differences between themselves and the teacher arose over translation, these might have been viewed positively as interesting points for exploration and discussion, rather than sites for battle.

The role of the assessment regime may have had some influence here. The teacher interprets the students' motives in terms of being solely interested in gaining marks. But how far has the teacher's assessment strategy contributed to this? Assessment for the course could be considered relentless, rather than continuous. There appears to be little room for experimentation or for drawing breath between graded assignments. One wonders how far the feedback from this constant barrage could be geared towards aiding learning, how far it could be adequately considered and absorbed by students. If there was a need for students to tackle so many translations, did they all need to be graded and (mostly) counted toward the final mark?

It seems that there is a profound difference of perception between teacher and students about the purpose and difficulty of the translations which were assigned. With regard to the Gorbachev speech, the teacher confesses that this was difficult, but he wanted to give students an insight into the possibilities of the Russian language, and he considered it reasonable for that purpose. Besides, it was good, contemporary, standard Russian. In making this choice, however, he may not have realized just how far below his level the students were, even though they were advanced students. If this were so, he may have underestimated the time and effort his students would need to expend in order to produce a good, literal translation. The lack of a context for the speech and failure to discuss the purpose of the translation would add to the difficulty. The teacher had taught the course only once before, and this may also have been a contributing factor.

For their part, the students apparently perceived their own needs in a fashion that made them more interested in making sense of the speech after translation into English. While they may have been wrong in this perception, it was a reasonable stance to take and one which the teacher needed to recognize and address. Were the students thus adequately prepared to undertake translation of this passage; had they built up to it and was it of a reasonable length and level of difficulty for them at this time? If the Gorbachev speech was so demanding and frustrating, could more have been done to prepare them for the task? These are the sorts of question the teacher might have asked before setting the exercise, or certainly after the incident occurred.

The teacher seems to have assumed, however, that the problem was lack of effort and hence the students' fault. The result was that instead of considering the possibilities outlined above and then trying to work such issues through with the group, he became defensive. The situation developed into a confrontation, with the teacher standing by his choice of assignments and becoming angry with the students. A good opportunity for clearing the air and also for the teacher to gain important insights into the motivations and understandings of the students was thus ignored. He knows that the students are unhappy and he senses that their general discontent goes beyond the particular assignment. But in simply blaming them for lack of effort, he misses the opportunity to find out what the source of the discontent is, and thus the chance to improve things.

Such an interpretation is fairly hard on the teacher. We know that he worried about the incident, how it arose, his role in it and what he should have done next. Had he approached and interpreted the incident differently, he may have been able to put to better use this concern for his teaching and rapport with the class. As stated previously, we might also bear in mind that he had taught the course only once before, and so he could still be learning about the appropriate level at which to pitch assignments. He was unable to make the best of the situation because his reactions were defensive and he did not consider the students' position to be legitimate (but based on a lack of effort). When he did make an accommodation towards the students he described it as a 'retreat'. Yet in making this 'retreat' and in rethinking the assignments which he sets for the remainder of the course, we see him implicitly acknowledging that the students had a point, and that their concerns *could* be accommodated without compromising his own standards. He thus had some cause to view the incident and its consequences in a more positive light than he did. Given his experience with the course this year, and his reflections upon that experience, one suspects that he might act somewhat differently under similar circumstances in the years to come.

QUESTIONS FOR PERSONAL REFLECTION

- *When you are faced with general discontent among your students about an aspect of your course, is your first thought to blame the students or do you try to consider what aspects of the course or of your teaching might be responsible?*
- *How would you go about trying to determine the true source of the discontent?*
- *How do you feel about negotiating at least a portion of the teaching/learning contract with your students? How could you do this, or do it better?*
- *Do you take account of the students' perceptions of their needs as well as your*

own perceptions of those needs in establishing a teaching/learning contract? How?

- *Do you become angry when challenged in class? If so, is there anything you can do about this? Have you ever considered that an angry outburst from a student may be a sign of dissatisfaction or frustration rather than a challenge to you?*
- *Does this case study have any other implications for your teaching? After having read and reflected on it, do you see any other aspects of your teaching practice or of your relationships with students that you might want to reconsider?*

A Disgruntled Teacher ...?

Case reporter: Mara Olekalns

Issues Raised

The issues raised in this case have to do with assigning blame when a class produces a poor assignment, the ways in which teachers may choose to react to such circumstances and the consequences for their relationships with the class. The importance of students clearly understanding what is required of them is to the fore throughout the case. Consideration is also given to what leads students to make a complaint about a staff member to a formal committee and what a staff member can do to avoid such complaints.

Background

The incident occurred at an Australian university in 1980 and towards the end of the second term of the year-long course. The female teacher was 24 years old and was completing her PhD at the time. The students were all 19 or 20 years old.

PART ONE

Although I had been teaching part-time for some years, I had become a full-time tutor in Psychology during the previous year. I had tutored in Psychology 1 and, at the end of that year, one of the tutors for the second year left and I thought that it might be fun to follow my first year classes on to the second year – which I did. It was during this second year of tutoring that the incident occurred. Although each of the three Psychology 2 tutors had responsibility for particular classes, tradition divided assessment according to assignment rather than class. During the year, students could complete five pieces of work (laboratory write-ups and essays), of which the best four marks counted for assessment. Each tutor had responsibility for conducting one or two laboratory classes and undertaking the associated marking.

One of the laboratory exercises in which students were involved was labelled 'Human Relations'. This exercise required students to attend two two-hour sessions in which they discussed and practised a range of communication skills. At the end of these sessions, each student was required to find a partner and interview that partner using the newly-learned communication skills. The interview was to be tape-recorded, and students were required to submit a written analysis of the communication which took place during the interview.

I volunteered to conduct this exercise for a number of reasons, the main one being that in previous years I had run similar classes and had enjoyed this style of teaching. However, I had been warned by the tutor who had conducted the exercise in the previous year that the subsequent assignments had been appalling – nothing more than transcripts of the interview tapes. I was therefore at pains to emphasize to the class that they should not repeat the previous year's mistake: I did not want just transcripts of the tapes. What I wanted was an analysis of the communication which took place in the interview, based on the concepts which we had discussed in the laboratory sessions.

The assignments duly arrived and I settled down to the task of marking the 100 or so that had been submitted. I was not very far into the marking when it became apparent that what I had in front of me was, in the main, transcripts of the interview tapes – the very thing which I had tried to avoid! My irritation continued to grow, and it peaked when I reached a write-up which presented me with a tabulation of the number of responses per minute made by each person. To me, this was only too reminiscent of the kind of statistics students would have supplied when describing rat behaviour, and it was meaningless in the context (a comment which I made on that paper). Overall, the level of papers seemed poor. I became progressively more frustrated and irritated, and I was generally giving low marks. At the end of this ordeal, I looked at my mark distribution: even I had not expected what I saw – I had failed about half the class and the modal mark was 45 per cent. What do I do now?

- *What do you think the teacher did next?*
- *What would you have done at this point?*

PART TWO

At this point I sought the advice of a more senior member of staff. The marks had been given out of ten and, by adding half a mark to everyone's score, I could shift the distribution so that the majority of students passed. This is what he suggested and what I did. I should add that, although the norm was bad, some students did exceptionally well. These were students who had spent considerable time with me discussing their interviews and strategies for presenting their thoughts in a report. As an acknowledgement of the difficulty of the assignment, I had made myself available for students from 9am–5pm each day for the two weeks preceding the submission date and I had been somewhat disappointed at how few students availed themselves of this opportunity.

Consequently, I was feeling quite irritated by the whole process and so added the half mark in the most obvious and ungracious manner possible. Rather than removing the original mark (I could have done this because they were written in pencil), I simply noted '+ ½' on each paper and gave a revised score. Further, as was the norm, I produced a feedback sheet for the students, making my comments about the exercise. It was quite lengthy and probably somewhat inflammatory. I can remember describing the students' efforts as being reminiscent of a cheap novel, not managing to go beyond 'he said ...', 'she said ...', 'then he said ...', 'then she said ...'. I also pointed out that I had warned them against repeating the previous year's errors and I then quoted about two-thirds of the previous year's feedback sheet since it covered all their 'sins'.

The assignments were duly returned and, with the exception of a handful of students who came to see me about their marks, I heard little else – for a while. One of the student representatives that year (Jill) was particularly extroverted and outspoken (and my guess is that she hadn't done particularly well on the assignment). The next thing that I heard was from another tutor who had arrived at his class early to find Jill suggesting to the class that they had been hard done by and that the matter should be taken further – to the staff-student committee. We then heard that a similar proposition had been put at a lecture. No approach was made to my tutorial classes or to me directly. What now?

- *If faced with these circumstances, what would you do next?*
- *Are your sympathies mainly with the students or with the teacher at this point? Why? How well do you think the teacher has handled the incident so far?*

PART THREE

The active student representatives requested that an extraordinary meeting of the staff-student committee be called to discuss the students' grievances. (It truly was extraordinary, as I don't recall any other such meeting ever taking place.) I was asked to attend, although the implication was that I probably should be seen but not heard. The meeting was duly convened. In an extremely articulate manner, one of the student representatives presented a somewhat lengthy list of grievances. I felt that some of these were just, while others were not. One which I recall was that students who had discussed their laboratory reports with me had generally done better than those who had not. This was seen to be in some way discriminatory. In general, however, their complaints seemed to be not so much about the marks as about the tone in which the subsequent feedback had been delivered.

Staff, in general, were not entirely sympathetic to the students' cause and some made comments to this effect ('You've been given your extra half mark; what's the problem?'). The second year course coordinator that year was the resident clinical psychologist, and it had been largely left to him to deal with the students' complaints. He was a true craftsman when it came to interpersonal matters. He listened (with many nods, mmms, and uh-huhs interspersed appropriately), stroked his beard, empathized and placated. Each grievance was heard and recognized as an understandable concern of the students. Nothing was done. The students' complaints were heard and the meeting was ended. There were no suggestions that anything more could, or should, be done. The matter was laid to rest there and then.

Postscript

In retrospect, the entire sequence of events seems somewhat bizarre. It appears to me to display all the signs of a classic escalating conflict: one in which people polarize quickly to defend their positions and don't in any way address the underlying concerns of the participants. That it should have reached a formal meeting seems, at best, unfortunate. Although nothing more was said, I am still left wondering about how satisfied with the outcome the students were.

- *How satisfied would you have been with this outcome? If you had been in the teacher's position, would you have done anything more following the meeting?*
- *If faced with a similar incident, what would have been your approach; what would you have done differently?*

Discussion

The main issue raised by this case concerns the need for effective communication between teacher and students. It seems the teacher considers she has *clearly* stated her expectations for the assignment and following this she expects that the 'disasters' of the past will not be repeated. However, from the students' point of view things appear more contentious, and there is a question as to how *effectively* the teacher has made plain her expectations.

While students have been told what *not* to do, it is far from clear that they have much idea of what *to* do. In hindsight, some examples or illustrations of what the lecturer required for the assignment might have had much more effect than her admonitions concerning what went wrong last year. *Telling* students, especially when this happens before they come to produce a piece of work, often has far less of an effect than *showing* them. They are obviously in a far better position to translate what they have been told or shown when they clearly understand the context, having experienced what is involved in the activity, rather than before they have taken any active part. Thus, although the teacher appears to regard their poor performance as the deliberate act of students petulantly ignoring advice they have been given, the fact that so many of them seemed not to have grasped the message the teacher tried to convey would suggest that this is not a particularly convincing interpretation.

Such a reading is strengthened by the fact that the only students who performed well on the assignment were those who sought further clarification and discussed the requirements at some length with the lecturer. Those who did take advantage of the teacher's offer of assistance were obviously introduced to a new way of seeing the requirements of the assignment by the teacher. One wonders whether, with hindsight, the teacher might have detected that the class as a whole was off-course on the assignment from the misunderstandings and comments of those who came to see her. If so, she might have made another move towards outlining what she expected to the whole class (perhaps in a circular containing a couple of examples) rather than continuing to sit waiting in her office, obviously annoyed by the fact that few students took advantage of her selfless act in making herself available for consultation before the assignment was due in. There is also a question to be answered here to the effect: 'Why are students not going to see the teacher when it seems they really need to?' In future, the teacher may want to investigate this and see why the present system appears not to be working.

The simple factor of lack of time may have played a part in a number of aspects of this case. It may have been lack of time which deterred students from visiting the teacher, and it may have been pressure on time which had a direct effect upon the assignment. If students were under pressure with a number of assignments to hand in, then this one might have suffered as a consequence. Merely producing a transcript of the conversation which was held could of itself be a fairly daunting task. Having taken the time and effort to produce this, students may have felt that they had spent more than a fair amount of time on the assignment, and have handed the transcript in as the assignment report. Late on the night before the assignment was to be handed in, and after many hours of work on the transcript, how many students would have recalled the teacher's words of warning a couple of weeks previously?

When the teacher starts to mark the assignments, she quickly realizes what has happened, but she tends to blame the students for not listening, rather than herself for failing to make her expectations clear. While her immediate response of anger is understandable, it is apparent that displaying her anger will do little to alleviate the problem or to help her longer-term relationship with the students. One feels that at this point she could have taken a more conciliatory line, perhaps accepting some of the blame for failing to make clear what she wanted (rather than what she did not want) to the class as a whole (rather than those who sought further guidance). There was then a chance to hand back the assignment before a mark was given, talk with the students and clarify the nature of her expectations, and give them the opportunity to complete the analysis and interpretation of the dialogue which had been missing from so many of the assignments at the first submission. While such an act might be seen as 'weakness' by some, the hope would be that the students involved would see it as an attempt to be fair and to demonstrate that some of the blame for the incident was being accepted by the teacher, and that at the end of the exercise, students would have a clear idea of how to undertake such a task should they need to do so again. One of the disturbing things about the case is that despite the debacle which ensued, by the end of the case one is left unsure about whether most of the students have learned the required skills which it was anticipated they would gain from the assignment.

When the challenge to the teacher comes in the form of a complaint to the formal committee, the teacher is quite reasonably disappointed that the students did not take their case up with her in the first instance. Indeed, most committees of this kind (or in differing circumstances, heads of departments) usually insist that the parties concerned try to settle their differences before entering a more formal stage of arbitration. One wonders if the students' reluctance to discuss the matter with the teacher had anything to do with the stance she took when she made some fairly hostile remarks on the students' papers. Indeed, she herself interpreted the students' complaints to be mainly about the 'tone' of the feedback she had given. A more conciliatory stance earlier in the case may thus have persuaded the students to have approached her, rather than the committee. Had they done so, the outcome could have been more positive from all points of view, as we see here a teacher who is willing to acknowledge some of the students' concerns as legitimate and not one who has taken a stance of rejecting all criticism. This adds to the irony of the case in that the open, free and effective flow of communication between teacher and students might have avoided some of the problems encountered during this exercise on the subject of communication.

QUESTIONS FOR PERSONAL REFLECTION

- *Do you explicitly discuss the objectives of your assignments and the criteria by which they will be evaluated? How far are students asked to participate in this process?*
- *Have you found it beneficial (or do you think it could be beneficial) to give examples of the kind of work you expect from an assignment? If so, under what kinds of circumstance?*
- *Do you generally tend to blame the students or yourself when most of the class produces poor results? Can you do anything to investigate the matter further?*
- *How do you react when the case is made or you see for yourself that you have made a mistake? What course of action would you tend to take and why?*
- *Are there any other implications or lessons to be drawn from this case which have application in your own teaching? Is there anything in your own teaching practice that you need to reconsider after having read and reflected on this case?*

Blue Moves

Case reporter: The person who reported this case wishes to remain anonymous

Issues Raised

This case raises the issue of how to respond to pranks in class. The incident described constitutes a breach of etiquette which accentuates the dilemma facing the teacher. There are also gender implications.

Background

This case study records incidents which occurred near the end of a course for about 80 students who were mostly 19 or 20 years old. The students were of both sexes, but the student who provoked the incident was male. At the time, the female teacher was 33 years old. She had seven years of experience teaching in high schools and three years at university. Three years was also the length of time that she had taught the course described in the case.

PART ONE

This incident happened in the mid-1980s in a second-year class which I had arranged as a seminar. The course was called 'Movement Development and Motor Dysfunction' and was taught in the Physical Education Department.

I had been teaching the course for three years and each year I had changed part of the content in order, I hoped, to improve the course material. In this particular block of lectures/seminars, the students had been divided into groups comprising three or four students each. These groups concerned themselves with the problem areas which the students tackled in the clinical situation. (Each student was assigned for the year a child with movement dysfunction and worked with that child in the clinical setting.)

Each group's task was to prepare in the clinic a video session which highlighted the child's problem. The students brought the videotape and 'case study' material which they had prepared to the seminar and, as a group, presented the case to the class. Each presentation was followed by a discussion lasting approximately five to ten minutes.

The incident

The group that was involved was last to present during its session and followed a particularly well prepared and interesting (in terms of the subsequent discussion) case study.

One member of the group gave the introduction. A second member of the group was then responsible for playing and commenting on the video. The equipment and tape had already been set up and the student leaned over and pushed the 'on' button. At that point the screen showed an explicit scene from an adult blue movie!

Hurriedly and with a joke, the student changed videotapes and the session continued, although the class had clearly lost concentration. The students had initially gasped, laughed and then become silent, and most students now appeared to be rather confused. What do I do now?

- *If you had been in the teacher's place, what would you have done next?*
- *What do you think she actually did?*

PART TWO

It was obvious from the class that the insertion of the video material was not appreciated. At first most of the students laughed with embarrassment, but they quickly realized the seriousness of the situation. There followed a rather stunned silence as the class turned to me and the student concerned changed videotapes. The planned presentation continued in a rather awkward atmosphere and I was glad, along with the class, that this was the last presentation of the session. At the end of the video presentation proper, another member of the group presented some notes from the case study on the child. There was little discussion at the end and the students left very quickly and quietly. I did not have an opportunity to speak to the student before he left and I recall being somewhat lost for words and without an immediate strategy. Reflecting on the incident the following day I decided that:

(a)   the student had intended it to be a 'harmless' joke and was not 'setting me up' for an embarrassing situation or confrontation;

(b)   although I had not confronted him in class, I would not let the incident pass without comment.

Knowing that I would see the student in the clinical setting, I planned to ask to see him 'in private', before the next class. By his attitude to the requested meeting, I knew immediately that he was not only sorry for what had happened but concerned about the class and about his future.

I decided to turn the interview around. After establishing why he did it, I asked him what he would have done in my position. Fortunately, he agreed that the behaviour was inappropriate and he apologized for what he had done. Interestingly, he was also concerned for the class! He agreed that he should not be given credit for his contribution. I agreed that this incident would not be considered in his final grade if he could prove his worth and academic standing in the other components of the assessment for the course.

The incident was never formally discussed again, although informally it is still talked about. The class regained its order and things carried on with complete normality. After the incident, one or two students asked me what I was going to do and I usually repeated the strategy of asking what they thought about what had happened and what they thought I should have done. I made it very clear that I thought it was inappropriate behaviour and that the student would not be given credit for his presentation. In all cases the students discussed their own perceptions and left our talks reasonably happy with the outcome – I think!

It is difficult to comment on an alternative scenario, but it may be argued that a confrontation at the time of the incident might have been more beneficial. Having had reasonably wide experience in high school teaching (even in some 'rough' areas of London), I am well aware of the different alternatives in similar situations. Teaching in high school, however, tends to be more personal, reactive and often more volatile, whereas a lecturing situation tends to be less personal and more delicate in terms of rapport. In my experience a public confrontation in the lecture would have upset not only the session but, I suspect, the whole tenor of the class for some time; after all, students are quite capable of making their own judgements and I have never been impressed by any member of a teaching staff publicly 'telling off' an individual student. But did I do the right thing? I'm still not sure.

- *How well do you think the teacher dealt with the incident?*
- *What were some other options open to her and what might have been their consequences?*
- *Do you agree with her thoughts about what might have happened if she had confronted the student immediately?*
- *Would you have done anything differently?*

Discussion

The issue in this case is clearly centred on how a teacher should deal with a substantial prank in class, although some important overtones which could have influenced what happened are worth considering as well. Just as with some of the other cases in this series, how individual readers interpret the incident will determine how they would have reacted had they been in the teacher's position. In this respect there is a range of possibilities to consider. Some might see it as a harmless joke, others as a challenge to the teacher's authority, and still others as a form of sexual harassment of a female teacher by a male student. The interpretation is likely to influence the teacher's immediate response.

Among the options available to the teacher were to ignore the incident entirely, to become angry and to confront the student on the spot, to joke about it, to accentuate it in some way in an attempt to embarrass the perpetrator, or to initiate a discussion around the incident. During such a discussion the teacher might have expressed her feelings about what happened, asked the other students about their reactions, and tried to get the prankster to explain why he did it. (She could also, of course, have reported the incident to a dean or head of department, but such an action would raise its own problems concerning abrogation of responsibility, since by such action the teacher would have passed the responsibility to someone who had not been directly involved in the incident.)

In any event, the course of action chosen would probably depend heavily on the teacher's personality and her relationship with the students. Alternative courses of action could have good and bad consequences but we may attempt to assess what would have happened in each instance. In the first place, the teacher was aware of the dangers of a public confrontation or the 'telling off' of an individual student in public. She was therefore unlikely to take this action. This decision was affirmed later when she concluded that it had been a more or less harmless prank instead of something more sinister. At the same time, she clearly did not consider it a joke worth getting in on herself, nor does the mood of the rest of the class appear compatible with such an approach. In that situation, even though the teacher lacked an immediate strategy, joking about or accentuating the incident would appear to have been out of character for the teacher.

She was embarrassed by the incident and could not simply laugh it off. Neither could she ignore the incident entirely and again we see evidence that others in the class felt the same way. She therefore took a middle ground. She did not confront the student at the time of the incident, when the situation was most immediate, but also when her own emotions and the general feeling of embarrassment were running high. She gave herself time to think about what happened and what she should do. We see evidence that even this initial waiting was worthwhile. The student concerned had time to realize what was happening to his joke and to be embarrassed himself, rather than being tempted to react defensively to an angry outburst from the teacher. Had the teacher reacted more hastily and heavy-handedly in chastising the student, the result may have been greater sympathy for the prankster from his peers. They could have been more likely to take his side if the teacher's power was wielded against a fellow student, and begun to think that, after all, 'it was only a joke'. The teacher thus took time to clarify in her mind what she was going to do. She was then able to meet the student in a less volatile environment and with the awareness that he was already contrite. Her delay and the approach she took had a number of beneficial outcomes: the student realized his own mistake without suffering abuse and the teacher was able to get him to see her side of the issue. One has the feeling that the student has learned an important lesson in life concerning humour: that it is important to think about what is appropriate, what will work and what will not in differing contexts.

Some will certainly disagree with the course of action taken by the teacher and see the issue of pornography being introduced into the classroom as very serious indeed. The interpretation of the teacher appears to be that the pornographic nature of the videotape was not central; this was merely a device to evoke a humorous response. Those who feel that the teacher has dismissed this aspect of the prank too lightly would feel it important to dispute the humour of pornography, to make the point that pornography can demean women and almost certainly to place importance on the fact that a male student in a position of less power had used this device against a female teacher (somewhat unusually) in a position of power. For those who would follow this interpretation there still remains the problem of how best to deal with the situation. Should the teacher give an aggressive response, lecturing the student and/or class on the evils of pornography, and underlining her overt position of authority and power at the same time? Should the teacher still respond calmly, defer action till later and use tactics similar to those used by the teacher in the case? Such a course of action might see the student responsible being asked to see himself in the position of a *female* teacher who had been subjected to this kind of practical joke, and the difficulties it could raise for her.

There may thus be differing interpretations of whether or not the pornographic nature of the videotape used to carry out the prank is central. Whatever the case, the teacher claims that her initial hesitation in responding was because of being at a loss for words and the lack of a strategy, but the approach she took (including the delay) was entirely in keeping with her own realization of the possible negative consequences of an immediate confrontation in the class. Although she questions whether such a confrontation *might* have been more beneficial, her assessment of the situation seems to be sound and we can perhaps learn from this that good outcomes from such incidents can be secured if the incidents are approached in a careful and restrained fashion. There is also something to be learned from the way that the teacher asked students to give their own feelings and interpretations of what had happened. By so doing, students had to think through for themselves what they would have done if placed in a position similar to that of the teacher. The teacher thus modelled a progressive educational stance in having students empathize with another human being and try to see the world from her standpoint. This is in marked contrast to an authoritarian model in which the teacher would simply have punished the student there and then and have told the rest of the class that the prank was bad, wrong or unacceptable. The difference between these approaches in this case has much to do with 'telling' versus 'thinking' and 'showing'.

The punishment which she actually exacted of the student was in keeping with her measured response but is somewhat more difficult to interpret. It seems that the student got no credit for his contribution but was given the chance to make up for the deficit if he could 'prove his worth'. Why this course of action was taken is unclear. The student (or the group) appears to have fulfilled the normal requirements of producing a 'proper' video for the seminar and of interpreting this, even though the atmosphere was one of embarrassment and there was little discussion. If the teacher's interpretation of the incident as a 'practical joke gone wrong' is accepted, then some might claim that having such a joke 'die' in public was punishment enough, and that it was unfair to use this 'miscalculation' as a means to discount work quite separate from the incident, and which would have been acceptable had the incident not occurred. On the other hand, those who saw the incident as more sinister would probably demand a greater degree of retribution. It is difficult to see that this would accomplish much, however, as the student appears to have learned his lesson already and any further action could well backfire and result in a souring of the relationship between the teacher and students.

QUESTIONS FOR PERSONAL REFLECTION

- *Have you thought about how you might respond to pranks in your classes? Are you aware of the possible consequences of various kinds of reaction?*
- *Do you think that you have sufficient levels of awareness of your own feelings, of the tenor of your classes, and of your students' perceptions of your personality that you could anticipate the sorts of reactions there would be to your response?*
- *After having read and reflected on this case study, do you recognize any aspects of your teaching or of your relationships with students that you might wish to reconsider?*

Goodies and Baddies

Case reporter: B H Ross

Issues Raised

The main issue raised by this case study is how a teacher goes about introducing highly innovative teaching methods in an uncongenial, conservative environment. Issues of teacher-student relationships, communication and the consequences of discrepancies between the perceptions of teachers and students about the purposes of classes are also touched upon. (Some of these latter issues are dealt with more fully in the case study *The Discontented Student* and readers may wish to consider that case before this one.)

Background

This case involves incidents which occurred in a newly-offered course on Electromyography in a Faculty of Physical Education. The male teacher was about 35 years old at the time; his teaching experience included two years at high school level and seven years at university. The students were about 20 years old.

PART ONE

I first read Carl Rogers' *Freedom to Learn* in 1976 while I was on study leave in Sweden. I had always been dissatisfied with the lecture and formal laboratory teaching methods in the courses for which I was responsible and I was keen to try a more 'self-directed' approach to my courses. So the year after I returned from study leave, I experimented with a small senior class who had enrolled for a 12-week course on muscle physiology. I structured the course so that students had a choice of several things they could do to fulfil the learning requirements of the course. They could opt for formal lectures and examinations, participate in and then write up laboratory work devised by me, devise their own laboratory experiments, share in my research project, devise their own research projects, critically review literature, or write an essay/review paper on a topic that I chose or that they chose themselves. They also had to state the grade that they were working for and make an individual agreement with me about what they would actually do in the course.

As I recall, none of the students chose to have a formal examination; all decided to do their own labs and/or projects. My lectures covered some theoretical aspects and demonstrated some of the techniques that the students could use in their labs. As the lectures were well attended, the students must have considered them important. There were 10–12 students in the class. All of the students were in their third or fourth year and they were highly motivated and interested in the subject.

My lectures proceeded smoothly with lots of discussion. I also had a great deal of individual contact with all the students in the laboratory. However, I found that I was having to give a lot of direction to most of the students, who seemed uneasy about having to plan their own projects and experiments. I felt that this was probably natural as none of us had experience with this type of teaching and learning.

Two particularly capable students worked together and had helped me on experiments in my own research. One of these students (Glenn, the 'goodie') was somewhat reserved but always asked sensible questions. He worked hard, doing a lot of the 'donkey work' in the lab sessions. The other student (Brad, the 'baddie') was outgoing to the point of brashness. He talked a lot, asked silly questions, avoided doing work in the lab if he could help it and complained bitterly that he should have to state what grade he was working for. He said that was his business and his business alone. I also regarded him as somewhat of an 'operator'. He had already asked me if he could use his project as part of the credit for another course. He also seemed to manipulate other students, particularly Glenn, to do the work and, perhaps, the thinking for him. This happened with respect to finding references from the library and producing ideas for experiments and for lab work. I did not like Brad very much.

Towards the end of the course, most of the students had completed their major projects. Some students had worked together on a project but had written it up independently. I marked these and returned them to the students in the third-to-last class. Brad and Glenn had done their project together and I felt uncomfortable about the similarity in the writing style of the two projects. When I compared other work by these students, I got the impression that Brad had used Glenn's material in writing his report. After much soul searching I gave Glenn an A grade and Brad a B+ with a note asking them to come and see me after class. Glenn was absent from that class, so I mentioned to Brad that I would like him to come and talk with me about his work.

Brad came to see me the next day. He was angry and accused me of bias. He also made it very clear that he thought the structure of the course was totally inappropriate for a university course, as I was not teaching; I was not giving the students the benefits of my knowledge and overseas experience, etc. I felt attacked and retreated by claiming that I was not biased but had felt that Brad's work seemed to rely heavily on Glenn's work. I was also prepared to accept his claim of independent work and to have his and Glenn's papers assessed independently. Brad refused this offer and, after more derogatory remarks, left my office.

I felt incredibly threatened. My colleagues at work had been sceptical of my teaching approach, so I now felt that the whole scheme had crashed. As I could not think of anything to do, I decided to wait until I had spoken with Glenn.

Glenn did not come to see me before the next class, but Glenn and Brad and all of the other students were at that next class. I handed out some marked work and intended to continue having students share aspects of their projects with the rest of the class (this had been the purpose of the previous two class sessions). However, Brad raised the issues of my marking and of the course structure, making it clear that he wanted the whole matter discussed in class. I was surprised.

- *What do you think the teacher should do now? Should he allow a discussion of the course structure in class?*
- *What do you think happened next?*

PART TWO

After Brad announced to the class that he didn't like the course structure and that he thought my marking was biased, there was an embarrassed shuffling of papers and I just wanted to jump down a hole. After some silence I asked Brad what he thought the real problem was. He made it quite clear that he thought the problem was me. My teaching was unprofessional and my marking too subjective. I was feeling so bad and threatened that I don't remember much of what actually happened in that class. But I do feel that the class mood was negative towards the course structure. They wanted the facts and considered that all this self-directed learning was just playing around. I don't recall anyone else complaining about unfair marking, but Glenn did support Brad in his claim that he had been discriminated against. Discussion of this sort continued for the whole 50 minutes, with it being agreed that Brad could take his work to another staff member to be marked. I was devastated by the rejection of what I saw as a successful way to promote learning, so I asked the class to decide if they wanted the next and last class to be held. They voted to cancel it. At the end of the session I asked any students who wanted to, to come and see me and I said that I would be happy to receive any anonymous written comments or suggestions for the next year.

No students came to see me. I received no comments in writing. All the students passed the course with a grade of B or better. And Brad – well, he still got a B+ for his project and for the course! He and Glenn both went on to do postgraduate degrees. I ran the course in a conventional lecture/lab format the next time I taught it and I didn't feel confident enough to experiment with self-directed learning again until 1985.

Since 1985 I have received positive comments from all students involved in the self-directed approach to learning. They all wish that more of their university learning was structured so that they were given responsibility for their own learning. However, most of them find the first part of the course unsettling as they feel that they are not getting enough hard information from me. It is not until they become involved in planning and doing their own experiments that they begin to realize what they are learning.

Postscript

About 12 years after it ended, I was visited by a student who had been in that course in 1977. He was about to take up a teaching appointment at a tertiary institution in another country. He wanted my notes and course outlines so that he could experiment with a self-directed learning approach to his courses. He claimed that my disaster of an attempt was the best learning experience he had had as an undergraduate. He, like me, judged Brad as a 'baddie'. Was he?

- *What do you think went wrong with this course?*
- *Could the teacher have done anything differently to avoid the problem which arose? What other courses of action were open to the teacher in the class where the confrontation occurred?*
- *If you had been in the same position, would you too have discontinued your experimentation with teaching methods for such a long period? If not, in what ways would you have changed the course or your actions in order to avoid the problems which were encountered?*

Discussion

Although the circumstances differ in many respects, we see in this case some similarity to certain aspects of *The Discontented Student* case study. In each of these a student attacks a teacher who is using an unconventional teaching approach and accuses him of not performing satisfactorily. In terms of raising issues about the significance of discrepancies between the perceptions of teachers and students concerning the purpose of classes, they are very similar indeed and the case of *The Discontented Student* should be read for further consideration of such issues.

In *Goodies and Baddies*, aspects of the course itself appear to be crucial to the events described. Here we have a teacher who is open to new ideas and keen to put them into action. As a result of having read Carl Rogers' *Freedom to Learn*, he introduces a course which encourages students to be self-directed in their learning, which gives the students a great deal of responsibility and a wide choice of learning activities, and which asks students to draw up a contract in which they specify what they will do during the course, together with the grade they are working for. The teacher has no experience of such methods, his colleagues are sceptical, and the system is very different from anything else to which the students have previously been exposed. This does not sound like the best combination of factors to ensure the success of a first trial of something so innovative, but teachers are often optimistic and enthusiastic and sometimes do not stop to think about difficulties which may arise. This teacher was obviously very enthusiastic about his new teaching methods and does not seem to have considered that some of his students may not have shared his enthusiasm. This appears to have been one of the main ingredients of the problem which ensued.

The action revolved around two students who worked together on a project as part of the course. According to the teacher, one manipulated the other, who did most of the work. The teacher observed this and other behaviours which caused him to admit openly that he did not like Brad, the manipulator, the 'baddie'. This antipathy may have shown in his attitude to the student and he also recognized that it may have influenced his grading of the student. We see that the two students 'worked together' on the project, but the teacher was worried about the similarity of their written reports. At this point we may wonder if any rules or guidelines had been negotiated prior to the reports being submitted for grading. There is no mention of the students having any say in developing criteria by which the projects will be assessed, nor of guidelines being negotiated for the amount of work which should be produced individually or cooperatively.

In some respects it seems as if the next-to-the-last session where the incident occurs is the first opportunity students have had to question the process of the course and to voice reservations. Up to this point the teacher has felt that the course was going well, but it seems his perception was not unanimously shared by the students. For a course which was to be self-directed it seems that the students have exerted little autonomy in terms of bringing out the problems they have with the course up to that point. When the problem occurs there appears to be no history of dealing with issues constructively within class to fall back on and the teacher simply takes the criticism personally. There does not appear to have been the development of empathy or the building of personal relationships between the teacher and class which is often the hallmark of student-centred courses such as this. In short, the teacher feels he has been doing his very best for the students and is devastated to find that they are not only unappreciative but also somewhat hostile. While he has offered them 'freedom to learn', he has maintained his own ideas about how and what this should entail and expected them to comply without demur. Much of this was almost certainly due to the teacher's inexperience with such methods and, to look on the positive side, this has provided him with an invaluable learning experience.

On the other hand, the teacher has exhibited many of the behaviours which show why he was able to run self-directed courses successfully after this false start. His offer to Brad of the opportunity for independent assessment of his work was praiseworthy. Also, he could have asserted his authority during his talk with Brad (and later by silencing him during the class discussion), but he did not do so. The pity was that his willingness to listen and discuss class matters with the students could not be channelled into positive action directed towards renegotiation and the achievement of consensus on how the course would work. Obviously it would have been better for this to have happened during the course rather than when it was coming to an end.

Brad is cast as the 'baddie' and, his personal characteristics aside, he does seem to have a very simplistic view of the nature of university education and of a teacher's role therein. With the combination of his view of higher education and his attack on the teacher, Brad closely resembles Violet Morris in *The Discontented Student*. However, while the teacher in that case focused on the attack by the student and seemed unaware of its wider significance, in this case the teacher is only too aware of its meaning and, if anything, exaggerates this aspect of it. It is in this direction that we can concentrate further discussion by considering what the teacher might have done differently.

First, assuming that he had definitely decided to proceed with the course as described, we might ask whether better and more open communication between the teacher and the students, bringing the insecurity being felt on all sides into the open, would have helped. Brad was probably not the only one who had perceptions of the purposes of the class that differed from those of the teacher. Could better communication have helped to bring Brad and the other students around? The problem is that there was probably not enough experience on either side for this to have helped during the first trial of the system and something else could well have precipitated a problem even if it had not been the 'Brad' incident. The question is open as to whether another incident would have had such dire consequences for the teacher's confidence and for his motivation to use innovative teaching methods.

Second, we might consider how the teacher could have done things differently from the outset. It might reasonably be asked whether, despite his keenness, he went overboard in response to reading *Freedom to Learn*. He may well have tried to achieve too much in one step and it might have been better to move more slowly, to make sure that he had his students 'on side', and to monitor reactions carefully and often, while feeling his way and gaining experience. Instead, he tried to put in place all of the components of a radical course, alone, in a hostile environment and at one time. This offered every prospect of being overwhelming for the students, for the school, for the teacher's colleagues and for the teacher himself. It would appear that the combination of his lack of experience with the methods and the uncertainty of what to expect, lowered the teacher's confidence so that when the outspoken student protested, the teacher exaggerated the significance of the incident and concluded that his course had failed. Because he thought his course had failed, he thought he himself had failed, too, and this was devastating. He did not get any support from other students or from his colleagues and was so discouraged by this experience that he did not try such an approach to teaching again for about seven years. It could be argued, therefore, that the incident with Brad was somewhat irrelevant and that if it had not been Brad it could have been something else. The main point is that the teacher was isolated and unsupported in his attempts to implement radically different and innovative teaching methods. He had not developed strategies to cope with dissension and to draw students into cooperative and productive negotiation of their own course. Despite the teacher's best efforts, therefore, it seems that, to the students, the course and the learning were still considered to be the property and pet scheme of the teacher.

It has already been noted how the teacher felt personally threatened by Brad's challenge and by his lack of support from other students and from colleagues, and that based on these factors he believed that his whole course had failed. It is unfortunate that the teacher appears not to have realized that there could well have been other sources of support. He could have had useful discussion and feedback from colleagues in other departments or from a higher education development unit or personnel instead of having to rely solely on his own impressions and on the negative reactions of his colleagues and of Brad. The support that others could have given might have been sufficient to tip the balance so that the combination of his trying to do too much and the negative reactions of students and colleagues would not have destroyed his own confidence and set his development in teaching back for several years.

It is interesting to note how much better his programme seems to have gone since 1985. The students probably have not changed much since 1977, but the teacher's experience, his confidence and his feelings of comfort with unconventional methods will certainly have increased. Fortunately, he was resilient enough to maintain his commitment to progressive principles of teaching and he was willing to return to them despite his earlier disappointment. A weaker person might well have given up for good.

In summary, therefore, had the teacher been fortunate enough to have available the insights which his case offers to us, he would have recognized two major points:

1. In introducing innovative teaching methods, it is best to take account of one's circumstances and environment and not to try to do too much at once. A small success holds more promise for future progress than does a big failure.
2. Teachers implementing new methods often do not foresee possible problems and experience a lack of confidence or feelings of insecurity when they occur. Most teachers should look for support from friendly colleagues, from other teachers who are trying innovative teaching methods, and from consultants in an educational development unit on campus if these are available. Support can help to keep the innovator going so that he or she is able to keep an incident such as the one in this case study in perspective and not let it destroy his or her confidence or commitment to innovative teaching practice.

QUESTIONS FOR PERSONAL REFLECTION

- *If you have been thinking of introducing innovative teaching methods, have you considered how far you might be able to move within the constraints of your own environment and how far you would feel comfortable to move? Do you agree that it is advisable to move a little at a time unless you are well endowed with experience, courage and resilience?*

- How would you go about overcoming the resistance of students to teaching and learning methods which are new and foreign to their experience? Should you collect materials for students to read on the subject; should you involve them in negotiating the process and content of the course?
- What resources do you have within yourself, your department and your school to help you if students respond unfavourably to a first trial of a new method? In such circumstances, could you learn from the experience without abandoning the good in what you were doing?
- Can you identify colleagues who would support you and educational consultants who would provide advice and support to help you persevere with innovative teaching practices?
- Are there any other implications of this case study for your own teaching practice?

The Unexpected Telephone Call

Case reporter: Peter Schwartz

Issues Raised

Teacher-student relationships and the roles of teachers in counselling students are the main issues raised by this case study.

Background

The events which are described occurred early in the 1989 teaching year. At that point, the male teacher was 49 years old and had been teaching for 22 years, although it was only his second year of teaching his course by the new method described in the case. The student in question was in her late 20s.

PART ONE

It certainly was unexpected. I was just finishing brushing my teeth after lunch and was in a room down the corridor from my office. I thought I heard the telephone ring, but I didn't rush. I knew that I had a diversion so that the call would go to the secretary's office if I didn't answer by the fifth ring. When I heard it stop ringing in my room and start in the secretary's office, I headed that way, toothbrush still in hand. The call was for me, but what a surprise it was to hear when I got on the line: 'Hello, this is Eileen in Wellington. I'm feeling low. Pep me up'.

Eileen had been one of my students from the previous year. I first met her when she was a second-year medical student and she was in a group that was assigned to me for a small group session on medical ethics. I found her a very forthright but thoughtful person at that stage but had little more to do with her that year. However, I knew that she was genuinely concerned about issues of medical education and that she had difficulty with some of her exams at the end of the second year. The next year she was part of the third-year class and studied clinical biochemistry with us. My department was in the first year of a new programme, in which we replaced virtually all of our previous lectures and laboratory classes with small group sessions that used cases and problems as the focus for learning. Each group had 11 students, and each had students over the whole range of performance from second-year final exams. Eileen was in one of my groups. Because of my enthusiasm for working with students and for our new system of case-based learning, I worked hard to get to know the students, to make them feel comfortable, and to help them learn. I had a chance to tell each of them individually and to repeat to the groups together that I considered each of them part of my family for the year, and I wanted to do my best to help my family do well. I also said that I was happy to work with individuals if they felt that they weren't getting satisfactory understanding of material from the small group discussions.

I got to know Eileen quite well. She was somewhat older than most of the other students, having been working (as a nurse) before she came to medical school. She also lived in what must have been a *de facto* relationship and had two children, so that sometimes she had to leave a little early from late afternoon classes to pick one of the children up from the crèche. She was an outspoken, hard-working woman who seemed to be prone to bouts of self-doubt at some times and euphoria at others. She was a tireless worker for her class (she was a class representative) and was very keen to discuss and work on educational issues. She seemed to do quite well in the group sessions, but from the things she said it was clear that she had some problems with understanding some of the concepts that I wanted the students to learn. I encouraged her to come and see me if she felt that she wanted more help, and she did. I learned about the lack of confidence that she had in her abilities and about her reluctance to say things in her group because she felt so far behind the others and because she thought that anything she said would be stupid or wrong or both. I tried to encourage her to slow down the others in the group, to get them to answer her questions, and to feel relaxed about saying *anything*, since unless someone says or asks something, it is impossible to identify misunderstandings, let alone correct them.

We also went through a lot of the material together and this either reinforced or corrected things from a previous session or prepared her for the discussion in an upcoming session. She got on well, but her mood changes in these individual sessions were very obvious. At one session she might appear very frustrated and keep expressing how 'dumb' she felt, while at another she would absolutely fly through the questions, answering correctly and with great confidence, and I would have to try and slow her down a bit.

The combination of approaches got her through our course without difficulty, and I know that she thought very highly of our programme. She was one of a small group of my students who came by at the end of the year to say thank you and goodbye, and she gave me a farewell hug. I knew that she was going several hundred miles away to the Wellington School of Medicine for her clinical years and that she was a keen volunteer for a new pilot programme of problem-based learning that was going to be used for the first time on two small groups of volunteers from her class. The programme was going to replace the highly didactic Clinical Sciences

Course and was being organized by a small group of enthusiastic teachers. It sounded like a very promising course.

I had heard nothing more of Eileen or the course in Wellington until this day, near the end of the first term of her first year in Wellington (the fourth year of her medical course). Now here I was in the secretary's office, with the secretary and a couple of technicians in the room, with my toothbrush in my hand, listening to: 'Hello, this is Eileen in Wellington. I'm feeling low. Pep me up'. What in the world should I do?

- *What would you advise the teacher to do?*
- *Is it the same as what you would do in his place?*
- *What do you think he actually did?*

PART TWO

After my initial surprise, the first thing I did was to ignore the others in the room. My prime responsibility was to Eileen. I felt very insecure, being so far away, not knowing any background to what was going on, and not wanting to run up a big telephone bill for her. I tried to find out what was happening to make her feel 'down'. I suspected that possibly some non-scholastic issues contributed, but I was hardly in a position to do much about those. Between exclamations of how she thought I was a great motivator from the previous year and that was why she called me, she gave the impression of being weary with her load and of moving back to her feeling of not wanting to say anything in her learning group because it would invariably be 'dumb'. I gathered that some difficulties had arisen with the new pilot programme. In particular, one very bright student in her group was taking over the sessions by answering all the questions, and this behaviour was being encouraged by the tutor. My own feeling was that this action by the tutor was inappropriate and unwise, and I told Eileen this. She responded that *the members of the group* had finally asked the one student to let the others have a go. I said that I thought the group was showing more sense than the tutor! I tried to reassure her about feeling free to say or ask what she wanted to and said that everyone would probably take a while to get used to the new system, but I thought that the tutors' hearts were in the right places, even if they did make a few mistakes to begin with. We talked for a while longer, I tried my best to get her spirits up, and she seemed at least moderately satisfied when we finished the conversation.

I still felt uneasy afterwards. I was worried that I might have let her down or missed something important, yet I didn't know what else I could have done. I did take three further steps:

1. I talked with a faculty member who knew her and had probably been as close to the role of a 'student counsellor' as there was in the medical school. He thought that a lot of her problems were probably personal, but he acknowledged that there could also be difficulties with the new course in Wellington. As a result of a suggestion of his:

2.   I talked with a senior Wellington School academic (who was in town that day and who was very interested in curricular matters) and told him of my conversation and my worries about the tutor's methods. He promised to look into the matter and to get a quiet, friendly bit of advice to the tutor.

3.   Because I still felt that I might have been inadequate in my conversation with Eileen, I wrote her a brief letter thanking her for thinking of me when she wanted 'pepping up' and hoping that I had been of some help in spite of my feeling inadequate for the task. I again encouraged her to try to feel more confident and to help her group overcome the initial difficulties with the new programme. I ended by expressing my confidence in her and in her abilities, and to reinforce that I enclosed one of those wallet-sized laminated cards (which I bought specially at a book shop) that have several stanzas of thoughtful, spirit-raising (though non-religious) verse. This one was entitled 'I Believe in You'. I wished her all the best and enclosed the lot in a special envelope from the post office. This one had two hearts and the words 'Thinking of You' in the lower left corner and a printed stamp that said 'Good Luck' in the upper right corner.

I wondered if I was doing the right thing and whether I'd ever know what her response was.

- *What do you think of the teacher's response and of his additional actions?*
- *What would you have done?*
- *What do you think happened next?*

PART THREE

Several days after I had sent the letter and card, I received a card in which Eileen had written:

'THANK YOU [in red, triple underlined] – your letter and card proved to be the turning point in a pretty miserable period for me. I had the 4th year blues (apparently so did a lot of other people, but I was so miserable I didn't notice!). Things seemed so hard for me, (being single, with 2 kids) to get to do acute nights and weekends etc. Babysitters are hard to find around the Med School – and the more willing they are, the more money they charge!! That's still not resolved, but you've made me feel better about my ability to sort it out.

'Thank you again – you're the best teacher I know, and the greatest motivator – thank you for being there.

Love,

Eileen'

I also had a chance about a month later to talk again with the senior academic from the Wellington School. He said that Eileen was apparently looking a lot happier and he had had a talk with the tutor. Things seemed to have turned out well, at least for the moment. I still wonder if I did the right things or what else I could have done.

- *What do you think of the outcome?*
- *Do you think there is anything that should have been done differently?*

Discussion

The prominent issues in this case study concern teacher-student relationships and the role of teachers in counselling students. While some teachers might not perceive the latter as an issue worth considering at all, those who take an interest in the welfare of individual students (as the teacher in this case) will almost inevitably find themselves being called upon occasionally to act as counsellors. And since most teachers have even less experience and training as counsellors than they have as educators, it is worthwhile considering some of the questions which arise with respect to the counselling role. A number of questions might thus be asked about the teacher in the case study, questions which other teachers may wish to consider in advance of finding themselves in a similar situation.

Why and how did the teacher get himself into the situation he describes? This appears obvious, as from his own words we understand that the teacher went out of his way to develop good relations with his students. By providing extra individual tuition, he was, whether knowingly or not, inviting students who took up this offer to see him as a potential counsellor should the occasion arise that they needed one. After all, on many courses the teachers are seen only fleetingly and at the front of large classes. Not surprisingly, then, students rarely know even *the names* of their teachers, let alone something of their personalities or their amenability to being approached for advice and counselling. This being so, teachers who make it clear that they value close relationships with their students and who make themselves available to work with individual students should be aware that they may be seen by some of their students as potential counsellors.

The environment which the teacher established could thus be seen as playing some part in suggesting that he could be approached, certainly on matters of work, but also more generally. This atmosphere and the close relationships he endeavoured to develop with his students might have suggested to the teacher that requests for counselling could arise. That being the case, he might also have considered whether he owed it to his students and to himself to develop his expertise in this area. Many academic staff act as unofficial counsellors, and it could be claimed that to do so they need no more credential than being members of the human race. Many staff, without any formal training, make excellent counsellors. However, every now and again situations arise where staff members may find themselves completely out of their depth. They need to be able to recognize this, and even in ordinary cases to be able to put in place normal counselling safeguards to protect both their students and themselves. Such safeguards would include having a source for their own support: someone with whom they can talk over the counselling problem they are facing, ask for advice, and with whom they can both rehearse and reflect. Often colleagues within a department can share such a role. In addition, many centres, such as those for staff development, offer workshops in this area. Teachers who see themselves entering this area might be well advised to avail themselves of such resources. However, this discussion is not intended to be a guide to good counselling practice, and so we will leave the topic there.

Instead, we will consider some aspects of what the teacher actually did and what else he could have done. The teacher was faced with having to deal via a long-distance telephone call with a (possibly) depressed student whom he had not seen for months, while working from an office where other people were present. Although he tried, was it realistically possible for him to find out in a short time exactly what was happening to the student? Should he even have tried? One of his options at the time of the incident was to refer the student to a counsellor at her own clinical school. Had there been someone suitable and had the student been happy enough to accept this advice, the outcome could have been equally satisfactory. But the student obviously saw this teacher as her preferred counsellor; he recognized this and did not want to disappoint her, regardless of the insecurity he felt himself. Given the personalities involved, there was little chance that he would have either told her to try someone else or declined the invitation to talk. He appears to have had enough intuition about what was expected of him that he neither gave her the fatuous advice to pull herself together nor confined himself to making soothing noises. At the same time, a trained counsellor may have helped the student to identify for *herself* the problems and possible solutions and would probably have listened more and offered less of his own advice than the teacher in the case study.

He seems to have taken a middle ground in his approach, which is possibly the best that might have been attempted in the circumstances. Even so, there are a few more questions we might ask. What if there had been an underlying psychological or psychiatric problem that should have been attended to? We have heard about the mood swings of the student, the pressure she was under and the fact that the teacher had not seen her for some time. In most counselling situations, time and face-to-face contact would permit the observant teacher to be at least alerted to the need for referral to a trained counsellor or therapist. The teacher in this case study really had no idea how serious the problem was. However, his involvement of a colleague who was 'on site' and who could presumably form a better impression was a positive step which may well have achieved a similar end.

But was it wise of the teacher to involve other teachers in the situation? On the one hand, this was a type of breach of confidence in his dealings with the student but, on the other, it ensured that someone in her own locale would be able to keep an eye on her and to investigate a possible problem that apparently affected other students, too.

Was the teacher being too compulsive toward the end of the case study? When should one stop? If sending a card was appropriate, was sending a card with hearts? Would flowers have been appropriate or too much? How far does it matter in this regard that the student was female and the teacher male? These are unanswerable questions, but it is perhaps better for teachers to foresee that their actions could be interpreted by some as inappropriate, before they make up their minds as to the action they will take. The chances for later misinterpretation and the possibility of manipulation by teacher *or* student in a counselling situation are rendered far greater when the teacher enters the relationship untrained for and naive with regard to the role.

In the event it seems that the re-affirmation of the student by the teacher was just what was called for. How often have we as teachers found that simply telling students that we have confidence in them, that they can do it and they will succeed, is all that is required to set them back along the road of achievement? It is perhaps a salutary experience to remind ourselves of how much time we spend telling students what they have done wrong (not right), how they have failed (not succeeded), where they are inadequate (not remarkable). In a similar vein we might also ponder how much of our conversation with colleagues dwells on our differences and on criticism of their positions compared to our own, rather than affirming the links between us and acknowledging and acclaiming their contributions. Taking a positive approach to relationships is perhaps something which we need to remind ourselves of from time to time.

The development of close and warm teacher-student relationships can confer enormous benefits to both sides. However, as this case study shows, not only do such relationships take time, effort and commitment to establish, but they raise the prospect of the involved teacher being called upon to take a wider role than one solely concerned with content material. While most such occasions may be unproblematic, they do call for a level of awareness and a capacity for development in the area, for the teacher concerned.

QUESTIONS FOR PERSONAL REFLECTION

- *Have you recognized that, in building close relations with your students, you may be inviting them to approach you over a wider range of issues? Are you comfortable with this thought?*
- *Have you ever considered obtaining some basic training for counselling students who approach you?*
- *In meetings with students where you are acting in the capacity of counsellor, do you watch for signs of problems that might be beyond your capacity? Do you have any support in place for yourself as you act in the role of counsellor?*
- *Do you know what student counselling resources are available on your campus?*
- *Does this case study have any other implications for your teaching practice or for your relationships with students?*

The Discontented Student

Case reporter: The person who reported this case wishes to remain anonymous

---

Issues Raised

Important issues raised by this case study include teacher-student relationships, the teaching/learning contract, communication, and some of the possible consequences when students' expectations of courses differ from what the teacher intends.

Background

The incident occurred in the late 1980s and involved a course which is taken at the third or fourth year level. The teacher was 30 years old and the student about 21.

PART ONE

Richard Harrison had some seven years of university teaching experience. It was his third year at this particular university and the second time he was conducting a class on Planning Law. On arriving at the university, he had expressed a particular interest in this subject and he was greatly enjoying the class.

Since the beginning of his teaching career, he had attempted, even in large class situations, to adopt a question and answer teaching style, encouraging students to ask questions at any stage and trying to draw them out by asking them about the material assigned for each class and working through hypothetical examples as well as decided cases.

For the most part, the class was going well. At the start of the year, Richard had explained how the participation system would operate and that a small proportion of the final grade for the course would be based on class participation. He always went through the class alphabetically, so each student knew with reasonable accuracy when he or she was likely to be called on. Although this meant that students needed to prepare for only some of the classes, it contributed to student security and avoided a situation where the workload appeared oppressive. If any student explained that preparation was impossible for a particular class, Richard was always willing to reschedule that student to the following meeting.

Most of the students did the preparation and made very creditable attempts to deal with the matters in class. Richard realized that this was not easy because the class had over 100 members, but several students had told him that their confidence had increased greatly as a result of speaking out and that preparation assisted considerably when it came to studying for exams. Richard regarded the examination performance of these students as far better than that of students he had taught in a more lecture-oriented style.

There had already been eight or nine weeks of lectures when one of the students, Violet Morris, approached Richard in his office. 'I just wanted to let you know that it's no use calling on me because I won't be prepared. I'm doing five half units and two full units this semester, so I simply don't have time to do the reading you require.'

Richard explains his reaction: 'I confess I was somewhat taken aback. To begin with, the programme she had described was quite unsuitable: it meant that she was effectively doing seven units for the first half of the year and only two for the second. (A standard load is four and one-half or five units and most students regard five as more than enough.) I could understand that she was overloaded, but this was of course no excuse for not complying with the requirements of each individual unit. I don't know what she expected me to say and I was unsure how best to respond. As other students had also decided that they were not interested in class participation, I decided to treat her as one of this group. "Well, that's your decision," I said. "You have to decide how to apportion your time and I obviously can't make special allowances for someone in your position." This seemed to satisfy her and she left, her mission accomplished. When she had gone, I checked my records and discovered that in fact she had been unprepared on both occasions on which I had called on her so far.'

The year progressed much as it had begun. Those who had decided to forgo the class participation marks avoided the classes when they were 'on' or blandly admitted lack of preparation. The rest for the most part ended up with reasonable grades. On one occasion Richard was able to ask Violet a particularly easy question and she managed an adequate response. Even in the second half of the year, however, she failed to participate and Richard had the distinct impression that she was not attending class regularly. Violet ultimately received 20 per cent for class participation.

On the last day of lectures, Richard concluded his lecture and was about to pack up when Violet approached him. 'Are we supposed to learn everything for the exams with no indication as to what is more important?', she asked.

'Yes,' Richard replied.

'Do you think that's reasonable?'

'Yes,' he said again.

'Well, I'd just like to tell you that I think your lecturing style is quite unsuitable. I'm not questioning your lecturing ability, only your style. I must have sat here for 50 hours and I've got less than five hours' worth of

Planning Law. I'm sick of sitting listening to other students making up excuses for not preparing or avoiding the question. I just wanted you to know.'

- *What should Richard do now?*
- *What do you think he actually did?*

PART TWO

Richard recalls his reaction: 'I was dumbstruck. This personal attack from a student who, on her own admission, had done no preparation for the subject seemed particularly unfair. In retrospect, I should have reiterated my initial remarks to the effect that I had no intention of providing a watertight, exam-proof set of notes on the subject and that the whole idea of the course was individual exploration and personal grappling with the subject in the texts and cases.

'All I said in the heat of the moment was, "Well, you're entitled to express your opinion." That got rid of her. I felt awful and indulged in much self-examination, but I couldn't help feeling that if she had played the game, she would have felt differently about the whole thing.

'When the examination answer papers eventually arrived, I was interested to see how she had performed. I always mark the papers blind, to avoid any suggestion of bias, and I didn't know which was her paper until I had finished it. I am sorry to say her assessment of herself was correct: she did indeed seem to have about five hours' worth of knowledge on the subject and it was undoubtedly one of the worst papers in the class. It was very much on the level of a school regurgitation rather than the thinking student's approach which characterized the vast majority of the papers. She was one of about 8 per cent of the class who failed the paper, the results being confirmed by an independent assessor. This didn't give me too much satisfaction, however; I kept wondering if there was some way I could have prevented the whole problem.'

By way of comparison, in her other full unit, Violet scraped a bare (C-) pass. In the half units which were examined in mid-year, however, she obtained uniform B grades.

- *How well did Richard deal with the situation?*
- *Was there anything else he could have done? What might have been the consequences?*
- *Would you have done anything differently?*

Discussion

This case study is about a teacher who has implemented a successful method of promoting active learning by individual students in a large class and a student who chooses not to participate in the system and then blames the teacher and other students when she fails to learn much from the course. We might begin by looking at the actions of both parties and consider some pertinent questions.

On the face of it, Richard's position looks commendable. He seems to be genuinely concerned about his teaching and wants to encourage students to be active and to participate. He finds that in his system they do better than in a traditional course and he likes his method. At the same time he recognizes differences among the students' interests, their learning styles, and their willingness to participate, so he gives them options: they know just when they can expect to be asked to participate, they can change the day of participation if it is necessary, or they can decline to take part if they prefer (although this means they lose the portion of the grade which is determined by participation). He recognizes that his students do not necessarily have to prepare for all sessions and that some students will miss out entirely on the benefits to be gained from participation, but he is willing to accept these shortcomings if it allows students to choose.

Still, a variety of questions could be asked about both Richard's method of running the class and the way in which information about it was conveyed to students. When and in how much detail was the information about class participation presented to students? If it was presented at the start of the year, did it sink in? In other words, were the students really aware of the significance of the choice they had to make, did they fully appreciate and understand how the course would run and what would be expected of them? Was Richard sure that everyone was happy with the contract? Is Violet's reaction representative of what may have been happening more widely, she simply being the only one brave enough to bring it into the open? Even though most of the students did the work and many found it valuable to prepare and participate, is it possible that Violet's reaction was not an isolated one?

We are also unclear about what the 'participation' system was really like. We get an impression of large class sessions that are mainly lectures, the teacher setting and controlling the agenda, with a component of the teacher going though the class in alphabetical order asking questions about the material. Could this have been seen by some students as too threatening and led to their lack of participation? Obviously, if Richard had merely asked for volunteers, he would have got only a certain group of responders, but if the *students* had been allowed to choose topics, or if they had had the questions in advance to assist their preparation, might this have been deemed less of a threat?

Like Richard, most teachers want their students to prepare for class, especially if the teacher will be asking and answering questions and going through material that should already have been made ready. Although Richard was trying hard to be 'kind' to his students by the approach he adopted, should he have been worried that even the virtual certainty of being called on failed to motivate some of the students to prepare for his sessions? Was it the previously mentioned threat that caused this, or did some students find that they were not getting enough benefit or learning from the participation part of the classes to stimulate them to prepare?

We can also ask many questions about Violet, especially since her behaviour is being seen through the teacher's eyes. What was her purpose in coming to see Richard early on? Did she expect special consideration because of her heavy load of other courses? Richard could not be expected to alter requirements for her alone, since he did not do so for any of the other students who chose not to take part or prepare. Was she just lazy, a troublemaker, or simply overambitious in her schedule of subjects? We have some evidence that her intent was sincere, for although she missed classes and usually was not prepared, on the one occasion when she was asked an easy question she *did* answer adequately rather than acting defiantly. But what was the origin of her final 'attack'? Was she still hoping for special treatment to get around her decision not to participate?

On the other hand, could it be that with this outburst we are finally obtaining an insight into the real problem and the second level at which this case study can be interpreted? It looks very much as though there was a wide discrepancy between Violet's and Richard's expectations of what should happen in his classes, despite his contract and despite the evidence of the sessions themselves. Despite Richard's intentions and warnings, Violet apparently expected Richard and the classes to give her 'the answers' for the examination and she believed that Richard had been derelict in not meeting her expectations. There can be little doubt from her examination paper and its style of answer that she and Richard did see things very differently, but of course at that stage it was too late to do anything to help the student. Richard thinks that if she had cooperated, she would have felt differently. However, it is possible that the main problem is not particularly Violet at all but a need for Richard to communicate via both words and actions to the students as quickly and as consistently as possible what he sees as the purpose of his classes and for his assessment tasks to give the same message. Perhaps Violet was only the messenger telling Richard about his contract and communication, and the issue is not just how to deal with one belligerent student.

Still, we *do* have the incident itself and the need to deal with the individual student. Should Richard have tried to follow up on what happened in any way? Should he have tried to do something about Violet's unsuitable load of units at an early stage? What responsibility did he have? It is very easy to understand and endorse Richard's stance and the actions he took, and most teachers would probably find it difficult to sympathize with Violet. But taking Violet's outburst as simply one example, the more general message for teachers is that the outburst may convey more than might appear immediately on the surface. It could tell them something about their courses, their communication with students, and possible discrepancies between their own and their students' perceptions of the goals of their classes.

Such an outburst, as in Violet's case, could be interpreted as a cry for help. Violet has taken on an impossible workload and does not appear in any way to comprehend the reasoning behind Richard's educational philosophy and practice. Perhaps because of the high workload she faces, she seems to want to adopt a surface-level approach of note taking, rote learning and regurgitation in order to stand a chance of passing the many exams she faces. Richard's course must appear disconcertingly 'open-ended' to her as she cannot get 'the notes' to learn and reproduce for the exam. Richard on the other hand is looking for students to adopt a somewhat 'deeper' approach to learning, where they work on materials themselves and construct their own meanings from the materials. So, although it is too late for Richard to retrieve a great deal from the incident right now, there is much that he could learn from it in terms of clearly setting out the conditions of his course in future years, and of trying, at an early date, to identify those students who are not surviving under his regime. There might be a number of ways of doing this: exercises run and marked through the tutorial system would appear to offer good opportunities, as would other internal assessment tasks set throughout the year. Having identified those students having problems early, Richard would then be in a position to offer them further help, again possibly connected with the tutorial system. Although such actions might be seen as an extra burden to Richard and his tutorial assistants, these fairly simple measures could provide an early safety net for those who have learned to play one particular type of educational game and are confused when faced with another, no matter how well explained it might have been at the start of the course.

QUESTIONS FOR PERSONAL REFLECTION

- *How much responsibility do you believe you have to individual students as opposed to students as a group? How does this belief influence your behaviour?*
- *If you are thinking of introducing teaching methods which are unfamiliar to students or different from those to which your students are exposed in their other courses, how will you go about trying to get the students to adapt to and accept your new methods?*
- *Are you willing to accept that incidents which involve individual students may have underlying messages of wider significance about your course or your teaching? Are you able to interpret those messages?*
- *Do you see any scope in your own teaching for providing mechanisms to identify students who are having difficulties early in the course and for providing extra support for such students?*
- *Having read and reflected on this case study, do you see any aspects of your teaching or of your communication with students that you would wish to reconsider? Are there any other aspects of the case study that have implications for your teaching?*

Samuel's Seminars

Case reporter: The person who reported this case wishes to remain anonymous

---

Issues Raised

This case study raises a major issue of dealing with a challenge to a teacher's authority and credibility by a senior colleague. Differences between teachers concerning their approaches to teaching, the needs of students and the purpose of education are also important in this case.

Background

The incident occurred in the mid-1970s during the first teaching term of the year. At the time, Samuel Groves was 31 years old and had been teaching for seven years in total. Professor Edgley was in his early 50s. The case writer notes that Edgley 'has no research experience or qualification yet holds a professorial appointment in the university'.

PART ONE

Samuel

Samuel Groves had been an above-average student in a professional course. He had worked hard during his undergraduate course and had carried out a research project in addition to completing the strenuous clinical requirements during his final year. Not wishing to practise, he joined the academic staff of the university after completing his specialist qualifications and a research degree. His appointment was in a 'pre-clinical' department where he was placed in charge of teaching a third-year course that reflected his research interests. He enjoyed the stimulus that teaching gave and spent hours informally discussing with students various concepts, theories and dogma.

The incident

Three years after his appointment, Samuel was invited by Professor Edgley to give a series of three lectures in his clinical department, in the fourth year of the course. As Samuel had taught the students the previous year, he saw this invitation as an opportunity to demonstrate to these students the clinical relevance of aspects of the pre-clinical sciences. With vigour he attacked the subject matter and prepared a package that: conveyed what he saw as the essential information in the first lecture, critically evaluated this material in the second, and then assembled a composite explanation based on his evaluation of the supporting evidence in the third. The students reacted favourably to the triad of lectures and, as before, Samuel found himself taking informal seminars with groups of interested students. He approached Professor Edgley and requested that the whole class be given the opportunity to discuss the subject matter of his lectures as he felt that in the informal seminar setting only a few students were getting the benefit of his experience. Professor Edgley made time available for four seminars, each taking a quarter of the class out of 'valuable clinical time', and he decided that he would attend the first of these seminars.

At the first seminar, Edgley seemed overwhelmed by what he encountered. Students were discussing what he perceived as sensitive issues and his hard-won dogma was being challenged. Near the end of the session, Edgley became defensive. He raised his voice and told the group that the 'facts' were as they were in the textbook and as he and other senior teachers had taught them. He said that Samuel was only a junior staff member and therefore inexperienced, whereas he was a professor.

Samuel tried to get the discussion going again. He sensed that he had lost the group. One of the group asked: 'What do we need to know for the examination?' Edgley's response was immediate: 'The facts. What is in your textbook. You need not worry about what Groves has told you as he will not be an examiner.'

Samuel tried to get Edgley to discuss a basic concept. Edgley remained silent and merely smiled. Samuel put forward several topics for discussion but there was no response. The seminar ended with Samuel frustrated; his credibility had been eroded and he still had three more seminars to give.

- What would you advise Samuel to do now?
- Would you have followed your own advice had you been in the same situation?
- What do you think Samuel actually did next?

PART TWO

The next seminar

Samuel prepared for the next seminar. He now knew Edgley's viewpoint but was convinced that the students would want better material than that which was in the textbooks. After all, during the previous year the students had consulted original references, had critically evaluated them, and then had discussed their views with him. Samuel decided that he would try to build on the skills which the students had. He went through the original papers yet again, trying to glean further evidence upon which 'the facts' were based. There were a few inadequate experiments. To him 'the facts' were equivocal and largely empirical.

The second seminar was poorly attended. Only about half the number that should have been there were present. Undeterred, he carried on. As he wanted the students to direct the discussion, Samuel introduced the topic briefly and explained his reasons for questioning 'the facts'. The students were slow in responding. Samuel probed them. Finally the students admitted that they were really only interested in passing at the end of the year and therefore only 'the facts' were relevant. They had heard about the last seminar and knew Edgley's position and did not want to get involved in personal differences. Samuel tried to explain that 'the facts' were based upon the results of inconclusive experiments and that from them, ill-founded concepts and prejudices had been derived. In addition, 'facts' were transient and most textbooks were out of date by the time they appeared in print. The group seemed sympathetic but there was no discussion, not even from those students with whom he had met informally. Samuel asked if there were any specific issues that the group wished to discuss with him. There weren't. Disappointed, he thanked the group for coming and let them go early.

Samuel was concerned about his failure. He discussed it with his head of department, who told him to 'get on with it!' Samuel pondered on what this meant and assumed these to be words of encouragement.

Each of the other two seminars was attended by only one student. Samuel was shattered. He had lost these groups and the class. He thought it was fortunate that this was not his third-year group, with whom he would continue to stimulate enquiry. However, word got around about the first seminar and about Professor Edgley's comments on Samuel's teaching. His third-year class became disinterested and the class representatives approached him, requesting that he give them only 'the facts' they needed in order to pass the end-of-year examination.

Samuel continued with his teaching style, challenging dogma and making reference to original articles. His peers tolerated but isolated him. They suggested that his style of teaching was more appropriate to postgraduate students than to third-year students – a view he disagreed with. Samuel considered that his approach was appropriate for all of his university students, even though many would eventually be clinicians.

- *What do you think of the outcome?*
- *How well did Samuel handle the situation? What else might he have done and what might have been the consequences?*
- *Would you have done anything differently?*

Discussion

The issue which is most immediately obvious in this case study is that of dealing with a severe challenge by a senior academic colleague to a teacher's credibility and authority in front of students. On a first reading of the case, many teachers would find it easy to sympathize with Samuel and to criticize Professor Edgley, the students or both, especially since they apparently refused to respond to Samuel's efforts to initiate discussion of the issues. However, a closer examination of the circumstances might suggest that, while they are not blameless, the students come out with the least discredit in this case study.

We learn that Samuel was a good student, a hard worker, and keen on research. However, his approach to teaching seems to have been heavily directed towards *his* interests and not necessarily those most relevant to the needs of the students. Even after several years of teaching, he was still taking the same approach. We see it reflected in his preparations for his guest lectures where *he* did all the work in preparing a package, seemingly in isolation from the rest of the course, and specifically to deal with *his own* pet ideas. The students found the material interesting, regardless of its relevance to them, probably because of Samuel's dedication and enthusiasm. His impression of the material's significance was such that he requested extra sessions for the students to discuss the issues and to get 'the benefit of his experience'. So in Samuel we have a teacher who is doing something interesting and challenging but is perhaps not considering the *needs* of the students adequately, nor the place of his own teaching within the larger framework of the course.

On the other side, Professor Edgley seems to want no challenge to authority or discussion of what he accepts as current wisdom. With his emphasis on 'the facts' as given in the textbook, he probably showed a disregard of the needs of the students equal to Samuel's, but his position was obviously quite incompatible with Samuel's. Thus the spectacle of two teachers in conflict was created, with bemused students looking on and not knowing what to do. When in doubt, self-preservation is a useful strategy, and so the only real concern for the students was conveyed by the perennial question: 'What do we need for the examination?' Unconcerned with their teachers' private battles, they simply wanted to pass their examinations. Since Edgley had control over this, and could invoke his position of seniority, authority and power, he had to win.

The means by which Edgley won were of course abominable and anathema to the ideals of a university. He would not debate or respond to Samuel's position; the truth was as he stated because he was a professor and Samuel was a junior and inexperienced. This was a classic case of 'the power of truth' losing out to the 'truth of power'. Professor Edgley had many alternative strategies open to him. He could have called for a short break in the class while he and Samuel sorted out what was happening and how they should approach the rest of the class. He could have let Samuel continue but asked for a period to respond at the end of the session. He could have called a separate session if he needed time to prepare his case. One has the impression, however, that Professor Edgley's position was not one of academic or scientific dispute with Samuel, but had more to do with the appropriateness of up-to-date research findings for the training of practising clinicians. Edgley was not prepared to start a debate on Samuel's pet research territory as he knew he could not win. It seems that Samuel had the position of power in terms of knowledge, and he had almost certainly rubbed this in by being deliberately provocative in his dismissal of the 'dogma' that Edgley and his colleagues were teaching. It is unlikely that this had gone unnoticed by Samuel's colleagues. Edgley's power came with his position and status and he used this unmercifully. Edgley chose his ground carefully and, once seniority was invoked, Edgley had no need to discuss the truth of Samuel's assertions.

Although it was one of his possible courses of action, Samuel did not try to talk with Edgley in private and this would probably have been useless anyway. Samuel would not have been able to convince Edgley and Edgley's message was already clear enough. Yet Samuel still did not understand that message. Instead of realizing that his case was hopeless and either abandoning the rest of the seminars or changing their content or style, he went into more study in depth in *his own* area, the area that he wanted to push in the seminars. He took no account of the fact that the course he was teaching within was not *his* and that he was being frozen out. He seems not to have realized that being 'right' is often not sufficient on its own. To convince others of his position he would have had to change tack and be more strategic. This he failed to do and so found himself isolated.

Without such a change of approach, and regardless of what the students had done for him the previous year, it was unlikely that they would adopt his position in this course, given the state of play. What was worse, when word got around about what had happened, even students in his own classes would not accept his material and approach any longer. Samuel had plenty of reason to feel aggrieved, but he also failed to learn from the incident something about the politics and power embedded in teaching. Had he done so he would have tried harder to integrate his views and materials within the overall framework of courses.

There is always a tension between the questioning and research interests of the research scientist and the practical knowledge and application of the clinician. In examining this more carefully and seeking some degree of synthesis, Samuel might have found a more promising direction than the 'debunking of dogma' strategy he seems to have applied to all save his own work. Failing this move towards greater integration of his views and his work, his other major alternatives appear to be to withdraw into his own specialism and wait for more sympathetic conditions to pertain or to seek niches within his own university or outside which would be more sympathetic to his approach. To the end, Samuel seems not to have learned from the incident and was still going ahead with his style of approach regardless of the consequences. He may survive if he does not mind being isolated, if the students cooperate, and if they succeed in the examinations. It may even turn out that his approach is right and he finally convinces his colleagues. But it will probably be a long and lonely struggle.

While it is sad that the students displayed a lack of interest in anything but passing the examination, their position is understandable given the circumstances. From the previous behaviour of the students as described in the case and from what we know of their abilities and potential for enthusiasm, it seems reasonable to suppose that, in the right conditions, they would do things differently. However, the conditions in this case study are anything but the right ones.

It is depressing to realize that such an incident can occur in an 'enlightened' institution of higher education, supposedly devoted to the cut and thrust of debate, academic freedom, academic tolerance, and to the power of truth, rather than the truth of power. It is very easy to sympathize with Samuel and his apparently 'no win' situation. Still, his response to the public challenge and criticism by a senior colleague by simply doing more of the same seems doomed to failure from the start. Had he been able to regroup and rethink so as to design a course which was acceptable to colleagues and students and which still incorporated enough of the material he wanted to include to satisfy himself, then both he and his students may have emerged as winners.

QUESTIONS FOR PERSONAL REFLECTION

- *Have you considered how you might respond to a challenge by a senior colleague in front of students? What would you do?*
- *Do you feel that you are taking sufficient account of the real needs of your students (rather than your own) and of the overall course structure in the material you teach?*
- *If after careful thought you were convinced that you wished to introduce a novel approach to teaching and learning, what strategy and tactics might you adopt to help move a curriculum, a course, colleagues and students towards change without causing alienation?*
- *Having read and reflected on this case study, do you see any aspects of your teaching practice that you might wish to reconsider? Are there any other implications for your teaching?*

The 'A' versus 'D' Project

Case reporter: The person who reported this case wishes to remain anonymous

Issues Raised

Considerations of when and in what circumstances to make exceptions for individuals within general rules are at the centre of this case. Other issues include teacher-student relationships, empathy for students, and the responsibilities of teachers to individual students.

Background

The incidents occurred during the early 1980s. In the Foods course described, the class comprised 55–60 students, but each student worked in a laboratory group of 18. At the time, the teacher was 50 years old and had been teaching the course during four of her five years of teaching experience. The student was in her early 20s.

PART ONE

Mary Harris taught part of a second-year course on Foods in a Department of Home Science. The course dealt with cultural, consumer and experimental aspects of food study and comprised four segments in all. Mary was responsible for teaching the segment on experimental method.

During the course, each student completed four assignments; the best three grades from these assignments contributed to the student's internal assessment (20 per cent of the final grade). Each student also carried out a project which she or he selected from one of the topic areas; the project was supervised by an appropriate lecturer and its assessment contributed another 20 per cent of the final grade.

The policy of the department and of the course team was to advise students in writing at the beginning of the course of the due dates for written work and of the fact that grades would be lost for late submission of work, unless an extension had been granted before the deadline, for a 'reasonable' excuse. Ill health or compassionate grounds would normally be accepted; in some cases, pressure from requirements for other courses would also be accepted.

The course was a required one for Tina Martin, a final-year student who wished to proceed to a specific professional qualification after graduation. In the set laboratories on experimental work, Tina had often arrived late with no explanation, had appeared disinterested and had performed poorly on the written work (mainly discussion questions rather than a normal laboratory report). Her grade for this section was 50 per cent.

In spite of this being her poorest mark, Tina elected to carry out an experimental project. She was late in starting the project and appeared to make little progress. From an oral report which she presented to teaching staff and students (as required of each student), it was evident that she had failed to control conditions for her experimental work. Much of the work also appeared to have been done out of normal laboratory class time. These problems were discussed openly, as was the custom of the class.

The report on the project was handed in late, without comment, so it was automatically down-graded (for example, B- would become C-). Mary considered that the report showed serious flaws and there was a lack of control in the experimental approach. There were also several omissions and errors in the way the experiment was reported. On the other hand, Tina had carried out a statistical analysis of the results (an analysis of variance) which was not normally required.

Mary always tried to make comments on students' assignments to show where they might improve in later work. In this case she made copious comments but in pencil rather than ink. The project received a C- grade, which was then down-graded to D for lateness. No credit was given for the statistical analysis since it was not a requirement, and poor results are not improved by later analysis. Tina made no comment when her report was returned. Her internal assessment mark, including this project, was just below half of the possible 40 per cent of her final grade.

In the final examination, Tina obtained a further low mark of around 40 per cent. Taken together with the low internal assessment mark, this gave her an overall failing grade, but she was eligible for a special examination at the end of the summer vacation. However, this would preclude her from entry to her chosen profession the following year, those accepted having to complete their university qualification before the end of the year.

Mary was aware that Tina would be penalized when she tried to proceed towards her career, but Mary did not feel justified in reversing the decision to down-grade the late project when the question was raised by the dean. (The original C- grade for the project would have given Tina an overall C- pass for the course.) Tina now claimed that she had had other pressures of course work and these had caused the report of the project to be submitted late.

Some days later the dean approached Mary and asked for more details of the circumstances of the grading. Tina had seen the Academic Registrar, and in 'floods of tears' had protested that the project which had been given a D grade had in fact been graded A when submitted as a project in a Marketing course.

The project was returned to Mary, who on re-reading it found none of her pencilled comments. She had the impression that many of the faults which she had originally noted had been corrected. However, the report still showed a poor experimental approach.

- *What should Mary do now?*
- *Should Mary change the grade on the project? Would you?*
- *What do you think Mary actually did?*

PART TWO

Mary did not change the grade on the project, believing that:

- If the claim for extenuating circumstances was justified, the case should have been made before the due date in accordance with the normal procedure. It was not possible at this later stage to check the claims.
- The same project should not have been submitted to two courses without prior agreement by the coordinators of both courses. This was done for some projects within the department, but only after full discussion at the beginning of the course. In such cases the project was usually larger than that for either course alone but less than two separate projects. A case had never been made for a project to be submitted in two courses in different departments.
- The reasons for a poor grade for an experimental report were still valid. Different criteria could apply for a Marketing report and in fact it was reported that the other department had given the student credit for her initiative in using a statistical analysis.

Tina missed selection for her chosen profession that year and prepared to take the special examination. A few days before the special examination at the end of the summer, Tina approached Mary in her research laboratory, saying she needed help with the material she was studying for the exam. It seemed to Mary that Tina was talking in a rambling and unconnected manner, indicating that she had a much more serious problem.

Mary was very concerned that she might have been the cause of this by failing Tina's project, but she was unable to leave her laboratory work. She suggested that Tina return later or that she consult the dean. Tina did not return and she failed the special examination. She was awarded a 'pass as a whole' for the course in order to complete her qualification, this being an option exercised by the department in cases where a student was one subject short of completing the degree or diploma, had failed that subject and the subject was not the major specialization.

(In the longer term, Mary also adopted the practice of making comments about students' reports in ink, usually on a separate sheet with reference numbers on the student's work, and she kept a photocopy of such comments.)

- *How do you feel about Mary's decisions and her reasons for them?*
- *What do you think about Mary's actions at the time of the special examination?*

- *Would you have responded differently at the time of the main incident or before the special examination? If so, how and why?*

Discussion

Although solutions to most problems in teaching are ambiguous, there are instances when a teacher's course of action looks obvious and indisputable to many other teachers. The incident reported in this case may well be one of those instances. Here we have a situation where it appears that the rules for the class were clear, they were communicated carefully to the students, and a contract (even if one-sided) was established. We also are given the impression that Tina was made aware of the deficiencies in her project during the oral report which she presented. We see in Tina's behaviour a series of acts which probably make her fate the subject of little sympathy, in that:

- she appeared to be tardy and disinterested and to produce poor quality work;
- she sought to excuse lateness in submitting the report of her project only after it was clear that this factor could make a difference in her being able to pursue her professional qualification;
- she submitted the same report to two different courses without notifying anyone or getting permission in advance;
- she appears to have erased the teacher's comments and to have made changes before appealing for the paper to be re-examined;
- she went directly to the Academic Registrar rather than approaching the teacher and department to discuss the matter.

In these circumstances, the teacher's justifications for not altering the grade on Tina's report appear to make sense and would be difficult to argue against. Her strict approach would probably be readily endorsed by most teachers.

Yet even in this seemingly straightforward case, it may be argued that a variety of other issues could be considered. In the first place, was Tina's disinterest and poor work an indication of problems with the *student*, with the *teacher*, or with the *course*? How did she manage to get as far as a final-year course and then choose to do a project in an area where she apparently lacked ability? Was there no possibility for deficiencies to be identified and corrected before this, or alternatively for stronger guidance to be given as to her best course of action? In short, has Tina been adequately and appropriately advised? We appear to have a student who has been judged over a long interval to be in danger and yet who is allowed to go further in a direction which is likely to get her into deeper trouble. The general question here refers to the role we have as teachers in maintaining a balance between allowing students individual freedom and yet clearly articulating what we see as the difficulties they may face and what we ourselves see as the course of action which is in their own best interest.

Of more moment in this case, however, is the question of the teacher-student relationship and the issue of empathy for students. While most teachers would probably have no hesitation in siding with Mary, we may also wonder if Mary might have proceeded differently had she been able to garner a little more empathy for Tina. The key is in the fact that the outcome for Tina is so finely balanced: the result of a *whole* university career (in terms of being able to proceed to the professional qualification), let alone the outcome of this one course, hinges on a *single* decision by *one teacher* on *one piece* of work. Simply reversing the decision and not deducting for the lateness of submission would have made *all the difference* between Tina proceeding and her not doing so.

Teachers who choose to acknowledge this significance might well feel uneasy about Mary's decision, no matter how justified. (It is clear that the Dean of the Faculty felt somewhat uneasy about the situation in that he or she asked Mary to review her course of action.) Some teachers placed in Mary's position may have wanted to go back to check the records on Tina from all of her courses and to talk to some of her other teachers. The fact that Mary's decision would have such dramatic consequences could have prompted her to make absolutely sure that she was herself convinced that she was being scrupulously fair. In doing this, Mary might have asked herself: Was it all the student's fault? Could the situation have arisen because of something about the teacher or teaching, the class itself, outside factors (recall that later Tina did show signs of psychological disturbance), or sheer weariness? Tina has made it this far – Mary might consider if she really wants to be the person to stop her advancing further. On the other hand, maybe it is just that no one else has had the courage to do what Mary has done. And if Tina behaves like this consistently, would she be an asset to the profession? In making the final decision, it is the fine balance of her having made it *so far but barely* that causes concern, especially in view of her behaviour in this class.

These reflections are not meant to suggest that Mary *should* have changed the grade, only that there could well have been more factors to consider than were immediately apparent. It seems reasonable to suggest that such factors could have been taken into account, in fairness to the student and in consideration for the student's future.

Some further questions could be asked about why the teacher in this case behaved as she did. Was part of the reason she decided not to change the grade of the project a feeling that leniency would be seen as weakness or as backing down? Did Mary feel that Tina should be 'punished' for her attitude during the course? Did Mary feel a little guilty in failing *explicitly* to advise Tina about her work before the incident, and in not following up on Tina's approach before the special examination? Mary was clearly aware of a major problem but did not leave her laboratory work at the time nor, apparently, follow up later. Would Mary handle things differently if she had the opportunity to do so?

These and the earlier considerations all relate to one of the major issues in this case: What *are* a teacher's responsibilities to individual students? How teachers answer this question will probably determine their overall reaction to this case. Some would say that the student brought her fate upon herself by what she did and, while it is unfortunate, that is life. Others would be more worried by the outcome of the case, and may have taken earlier steps to avoid the situation which arose. What either group would make of the actual outcome (the student was given a 'pass as a whole' despite failing the special examination) is also worth considering.

In the final analysis, it would not be surprising if this case study leaves some teachers feeling uneasy, especially with regard to the student's point of view never clearly coming through. Consideration of the issues in this case may thus heighten awareness and prompt teachers to think carefully about what they would do in a similar situation.

QUESTIONS FOR PERSONAL REFLECTION

- *Do you have a position on the issue of the extent of a teacher's responsibility to individual students? Can you justify it? How far is your declared position reflected in your actual behaviour?*
- *When faced with a decision about applying 'the rules' to individuals, do you tend to take an extreme position automatically? Are there factors that you should consider that would moderate your approach?*
- *Do you feel that you really have empathy for your students? How do you know? How much would you let it influence your approach to decisions on issues similar to the one raised in this case study?*
- *How much would your reaction to a student's behaviour and attitude influence any decisions you made about that student's work? Can you justify that influence?*
- *Are there any other implications for your teaching to be derived from this case? Having reflected on the case, would you want to reconsider the way you relate to individual students or the factors you would take into account in reaching decisions that would affect individual students?*

Barry's Field Trip

Case reporter: Graham Webb

Issues Raised

The overriding issue in this case is how far a teacher can attend to the needs of an individual student. The case describes a teacher wondering whether to allow a student who does not fit the standard mould to follow a programme which is somewhat different from the norm. The teacher must consider how to weigh such factors as fairness to the other students in the class, the opinions of other teachers in the department, grading of the alternative programme, and the view of the external examiner.

Background

The field trip in this case study was an integral part of the Geography degree course of a university in Northern Ireland. During the ten days of the field trip (which occurred about two-thirds of the way through the teaching year), the students had time to look around, but much of the time was spent in collecting data for small group projects. The atmosphere was very informal, with students and teachers working collaboratively. The teacher was male and 26 years old at the time; he had been teaching for three years overall, and two years on this particular course. Barry, the student, was about 20 years old when the events took place (in the mid-1970s).

PART ONE

It was getting late and the bar was about to close. I had the night to sleep on it but in the morning I would have to make a decision. I finished my drink and went to bed.

The problem was Barry. Actually there wasn't a real problem at all, as I could simply do nothing and everything would continue normally. The problem was of my own making. We were in the second week of a Geography field trip to Amsterdam. I was again leading the trip; there was a younger, recently appointed member of staff along to help and 25 second-year undergraduate students. Barry was one of the students.

Thinking back, it now seems obvious that from early in the trip, Barry was very taken with Amsterdam. For him, as for most of the students, this was the first experience outside of Ireland. Barry was quiet and reflective but he could also be very funny, with an effective and inventive wit. He was well liked by the other students, although somewhat overshadowed by the four or so dominant comedians, who always seemed to lead the group. I had been talking to one of these students the previous night, and he had told me that Barry was writing poetry and prose about his experiences in Amsterdam. I was quite surprised by this and the next day broached the subject with Barry.

Barry was quite happy to show me what he had written, together with a couple of sketches he had drawn and photographs he had taken. I was immediately impressed by one of the poems. I thought it was great. It described a part of the city we had been in a couple of days previously; it caught the mood and atmosphere in an uncanny way. The other poem he had written I thought was all right, but the prose was not particularly good. He talked a little about how much he was enjoying the trip and how he liked wandering about alone in the various districts, seeing how the urban structure and function, the people and the atmosphere could change dramatically within a couple of streets. He was not effusive about this at all but quiet, seemingly a little embarrassed about talking this way and at times struggling for words.

It was later in the day that the idea occurred to me. We would be measuring and counting all kinds of things during our next two days in the city, with students organized into small groups and pairs, making their way around independently and returning to do statistical analyses of the data during the late afternoon and evening. Why not ask Barry if he would like to take these days to continue his wanderings and writings, and to include these writings in his field report as a substitute for the other activities? What a great idea!

Almost immediately I began to see problems. I had not even asked Barry if he would like to do this kind of thing. Would he feel pressured? Would he be interested? If he did want to do it, what would I tell the other students? Was it fair to them for Barry to be doing something so different? I had not given any of them a similar opportunity. And what would I say to the other lecturer on the trip? Could I justify having a student not complete part of the field course curriculum, especially for such an 'airy fairy' reason? Further, the field report counted towards the marks for the end of the second year and eventually, to a small extent, for the final degree. How could I mark this part of Barry's field report if he did take it on? All assignments were also double marked, so even if I did manage to mark such a section, could I justify the marking to one of my colleagues? And what about the external examiner? He could, and fairly frequently did, look at field reports. These were the issues I was pondering as I finished my drink and went to bed.

Next morning at the breakfast table, I was with a group of students talking over transport arrangements for the day. As I finished breakfast, I noticed another group of students by the window, getting up to go. Barry was left alone at the table, finishing his coffee. Should I go over and join him?

- *Would you have approached Barry at this point? Why or why not?*
- *If you would have approached Barry, how would you feel about suggesting the alternative scheme of work to him even though you knew there were some problems associated with it which you had not yet thought through, let alone resolved?*

PART TWO

I went over and outlined my idea to Barry. He was interested in having a go and agreed to write up whatever he produced in the field report.

When the report came in, Barry had produced what I thought was some patchy work. The original poem was still the best, but there was now a wider range with differing textures and tones. I asked a colleague in the Literature Department to have a look, but he was fairly neutral: neither overly praising nor criticizing. A colleague in my own department was more positive – he had taken the Amsterdam field trip before and appreciated what Barry had written. Between the two of us we agreed on a mark which, in conjunction with the rest of the report, just about put Barry into the top 30 per cent for the assignment. I showed the external examiner the report at the end of the year. He didn't see what all the fuss was about but quite liked the poems and was happy enough with what I had done.

The other students were interested in what Barry had produced. They didn't see any problem in Barry doing something different either – 'we couldn't and wouldn't want to do something like that' seemed to be the general feeling. If anything, they seemed to take it as a corporate compliment that one of them had produced something unusual.

I think Barry benefited from the experience, although, as I have said, he was never effusive. I do think that he appreciated his own individuality having been recognized. It was an important event for me, too, in that since then I have been less afraid to let students out of the content straitjacket and to let them experiment with discovering their own individuality. In fact, my courses are nowadays basically self-directed.

Interestingly, a few years after this, academic geography took a swing away from the then current approach of 'geography as science', with the heavy use of statistics, towards a humanistic perspective. Studies of literature and art, and the evocation of place by a variety of authors and artists came into vogue.

- *Was the outcome to this case as you had expected? If not, what did you expect to happen?*
- *If faced with similar circumstances, how would you have acted; what would you have done differently?*

Discussion

This case focuses on a teacher trying to decide whether not only to allow, but actively to encourage, a second-year student to follow up on an area in which he has shown an interest, but which is outside of the normal curriculum to be followed by his classmates. There are several possible consequences of the decision the teacher has to make.

The consequences for the student are of course not greatly elaborated, as the case is written from the teacher's standpoint. This being said, however, the teacher's impression is that Barry appreciated the opportunity to follow up a personal interest he had developed and to have his individuality and individual approach recognized. At least we know that Barry took the opportunity which was offered to him whereas he would presumably have refused had he been reluctant to do so. Presumably, too, there could have been some negotiation between student and teacher as to what exactly Barry would do, what he would produce, what he would miss from not following the normal set of activities and what could be the repercussions for grading. There may well have been potential areas of difficulty for Barry here and also in the fact that he was being singled out for special treatment. One such danger was that this could cause some resentment or even isolation from his peers if they saw him gaining special favour or an unfair advantage. This leads us into the consequences for the other students.

The other students appear not to have taken Barry's special treatment at all negatively, but instead to have felt in some ways complimented by it. This may not necessarily have been the case, however, and the thought that he was being unfair to the other students obviously crossed the teacher's mind. Indeed, it *would* have been fairer if he had offered the opportunity to pursue projects in areas of their own interest to *all* of the students. This the teacher did not do, and he could be faulted for not doing so, even though in this particular case there does not appear to have been any resentment from the other students. There is a general tension here which can never be fully resolved. If 'fairness' is taken to mean 'equal treatment', then the more one caters to the needs and aspirations of a particular individual, the more one is drawn from 'equal treatment'. It could and perhaps should be argued that every individual should be encouraged to attain his or her full potential and to follow an autonomous and self-directed path through the curriculum. For the most part, however, the 'industrialization' of higher education has tended to make provision for the individual subservient to the need for standardization required by a mass system. Opportunities for individual attention are thus the exception rather than the norm, and the teacher wishing to encourage a student along a different path may simply have to accept that he or she may be open to the accusation of treating a particular student unfairly.

This latter point also touches on the issue of who it is that suggests the individualized activity or programme. The notion of acting fairly towards all students is in some ways alleviated if the student comes to the teacher asking to pursue an individual activity. The teacher in that situation can be seen as merely reactive; the decision has been thrust upon the teacher. But when it is the teacher who instigates the different activity, it is perhaps more difficult for the teacher to rationalize this action. However, most teachers well know that sometimes, as in the present case, an opportunity presents itself which needs to be grasped there and then. To some extent teachers have to take chances and to accept the risks associated with their decisions; teaching without taking chances could be a formula for sterility, conformity, mediocrity.

One of the interesting aspects of this case is that the teacher saw all manner of problems and consequences which could follow from his action before he suggested the idea to Barry. Had the teacher agonized over these and tried to find watertight solutions before approaching Barry, he would probably never have made the suggestion. In any act of educational innovation or creativity (and this case represents no more than a tiny example), risks are taken, and rationalizations as to why the risks should *not* be taken are always available and often seductive. Any one of the reasons that the teacher rehearsed could have been used to justify not making the move. These included not knowing: if the suggestion would embarrass Barry; if Barry would be interested; if the other students would be resentful; if the project could be marked; if colleagues would be antagonistic; if the external examiner would be antagonistic. In fact, each of these concerns proved of little consequence, but the *thought* of all the things which are unknown, or that can go wrong, probably stifles more educational innovation and creativity than the actual conditions themselves.

The consequences for the teacher were probably more profound than for Barry or anyone else. The teacher was relatively young and inexperienced and the incident made an impression upon him as it was the first time that he had tried to accommodate the individuality of a student within the curriculum. Small episodes such as this one often assume a dispropor-tionate role in a teacher's development, and in fact the teacher reports how his teaching has changed so that his courses are now self-directed. It may also be noted that the teacher was fortunate enough to receive support from one of his colleagues. This took the form of moral support and encouragement but also the more tangible support of giving a second opinion of the mark Barry should gain. When a teacher is apprehensively trying something different (and the full consequences of change can seldom be foreseen), such encouragement and support may be of crucial importance to the teacher concerned.

Finally, the fact that comment is made on the way that the discipline of Geography changed over the years following the incident is interesting. By allowing creativity, exploration, autonomy and difference to be manifested by their students, teachers allow for a process of change and questioning which may be seen as the life-blood of knowledge. It could forcefully be argued that an insistence upon a set, predetermined and rigid curriculum goes against the very nature of the way knowledge changes and develops.

QUESTIONS FOR PERSONAL REFLECTION

- *Do you ever allow students to express their individuality in any of your courses? Do you ever encourage them to do so?*
- *Can you think of a time when you have considered doing something creative or innovative in one of your courses but produced rationalizations as to why you should not do so? If so, how well founded were your rationalizations?*
- *How do you react towards colleagues who try educational innovations? Are you often interested and supportive, or diffident and dismissive?*
- *Are there any other implications or lessons to be drawn from this case which have application in your own teaching? Is there anything in your own teaching practice that you need to reconsider after having read and reflected on this case?*

The Late Assignments

Case reporter: Alexander Sibbald

Issues Raised

The main issue raised by this case is whether or how to penalize students who submit late assignments. Reasons for having a penalty system are advanced and discussed, together with the consequences of such a system for rapport between the teacher and class. The nature of the contract between teacher and students is raised as is the degree to which students should participate in its negotiation and implementation, and the need for monitoring of the contract to take place.

Background

The Personnel Management course featured in this case was taught in the late 1980s at the University of the South Pacific. The Scottish male teacher was 49 years old at the time and had taught the course for two years. He had nine years of teaching experience in polytechnics and universities in Scotland, Fiji and New Zealand. Most of the students were about 19 years old, but the older ones referred to in the case were in their mid- to late-30s.

PART ONE

I had taught at the University of the South Pacific, based in Suva, Fiji, for the previous four semesters. My teaching had caused no problems at all. I had a successful format and stuck to it. In the next semester, I was teaching Personnel Management to a second-year undergraduate class of about 50 students. They comprised mainly Polynesian, Melanesian and Micronesian indigenous students, with a fair number of Fijian Indians and a small group of Fijian Chinese and mixed-race people.

At the commencement of the class I carefully explained my policy of penalizing assignments which were handed in late and tests which were missed. There were three main reasons for this. First, other students who had got assignments in on time and had sat the tests would be penalized if I accepted late submissions or alternative test dates without any deduction. Second, since the students were taking a management major, they had to learn to manage their time. Last, assignments were returned to students quickly, and late submissions would lengthen this turn-around time. There were no complaints or comments from the class. This policy was merely a continuation of my previous successful practice. Students accepted it as fair.

The system worked on the basis that one mark was subtracted for each day the written assignment was late. Missed class tests could not be taken at another time and thus received no marks. I had a reputation for being tough but fair, and for running a challenging course.

Students were graded on the basis of equal weighting for course work and final examination. To pass the course they had to accumulate at least 50 per cent from the combination of course-work and final exam, but they had to get at least 40 per cent on the final examination. The course work component was based on two multiple-choice tests worth 10 per cent each; tutorial participation which counted for 15 per cent and comprised ten small assignments which were handed in at the tutorials; and a written assignment valued at 15 per cent. The final exam also attracted 50 per cent. The written assignment was set in the second week of the semester and had to be submitted by the Friday of the seventh week.

During the first part of the semester, my relationship and rapport with the students was good. The first test was taken by all of the students, except one absentee, in week six. He offered no excuses and made no complaint, even though I had made the point that non-attendance would mean no mark.

On the last day for submission of the written assignment, a Western Samoan student came to see me in my office. He said that he had been busy and could not hand his essay in till the following Tuesday. I told him that was his prerogative, but this would mean a loss of three marks. He immediately became very abusive and hostile, behaviour which was untypical of Island students. He said that I was a very uncaring person and was being unreasonably hard. Other lecturers accepted late assignments so why not me? His comments hurt me because students often came to me for advice and help, which were readily given. My reaction was to keep very calm and again explain my reasons for the penalty. Within a minute or two he had stormed out of the office, muttering that he would get me put right. My records showed that he was a poor attender at lectures and tutorials.

The following week was the mid-semester break. On that Wednesday, another student came to see me in my office to plead her case for no penalty for late submission. A Fijian Indian, she explained that she had to go to her father-in-law's funeral on the previous Friday and had not returned home till Tuesday. She would need another four days to submit her assignment. I sympathized with her but again explained why the essay would attract a penalty. In so doing I also said that I had just refused an extension to another student, and that in fact eight other people had not put their assignments in on time. Since I had no way of assessing the merits of different excuses and was unable to check their validity, it seemed to me the fairest way was to treat everyone the same. As I said to her, 'Students never request that the final exam be postponed for them, so what is different about course work?' I also made the point that my system did allow for the overall mark to be adjusted in the light of circumstances, once all the semester scores had been examined and considered. My final comment was to remind her that the assignment had been handed out in week two. She accepted my explanations and reasons, although she was not very happy with them.

Over the next three weeks of the second half of the semester, I could sense that the mood of the class had changed. Pacific Islanders are normally very quiet and passive in class, but this was ridiculous. Some of them were not attending tutorials but were handing in their tutorial assignments via classmates, and they were thus not given a mark for participation. The Western Samoan student was prominent in this behaviour, along with three of his countrymen. They were most upset at being told that the idea of the tutorial was to present their mini essay and participate in discussion, and thus they could not get a mark for these missed attendances. They did not think this action was justified. I reminded them of my comments at the first lecture, when they had had an opportunity to comment about the assessment procedure but had chosen not to do so.

The results of the first class test and the written assignment were not terribly good, even when making allowances for late submissions. I realized that many of the other eight students who had submitted late assignments were now moaning and starting to be disruptive, and two mature Fijian students, a man and a woman, were angry at the poor marks given to them for their assignment and tutorials. I carefully explained the reasons for the scoring, but this failed to pacify them. My relationships with them had previously been excellent but now, in class, the man became antagonistic and hostile. These incidents happened about six months after the second military coup in Fiji, although I couldn't be sure that the two events were related. Things were going from bad to worse.

By the end of the fourth week after the mid-semester break I was really feeling awful and was wondering how best to retrieve the situation and to get back to the previous very good relationship with the class. Lecturing to the whole group was a strain, but the tutorials proved more stressful. It was like drawing blood out of a stone, only worse.

The second test was to be held in two weeks and I feared what would happen. Also, the final exam would be given two weeks after the end of the semester, and I didn't seem to be getting through to them. Was there going to be a third coup, a takeover of the Personnel Management class?

I was now getting really distraught. My next lecture was three days away, so I decided to get a grip on myself and consider carefully all of the options open to me. What should I do now?

- *What do you think the teacher did next?*
- *What would you have done at this point?*

PART TWO

My next meeting with the class was on the following Monday. It was a double lecture of two periods, 50 minutes each. By the Sunday evening I had decided what to do. The lecture was one of the best I delivered that year. It seemed to go down very well with the class. Attendance at lectures was voluntary and about 80 per cent of the students were present. I deliberately finished the lecture about five minutes before the end of the second period, having given the students a ten-minute break mid-way through the session. My next comments to the class were roughly along the following lines and were given without warning:

'Before you leave I'd like to say a few words to the class. If any of your colleagues are absent please let them know what I said. These comments are made as a colleague and a friend rather than as an authority figure.

'I've got the very strong impression from your behaviour and attitudes that you are very displeased about certain aspects of the course. This gives me concern. I'd like to discuss these problems with you in a frank and open way so that we can sort them out to everyone's satisfaction.

'You probably know that some students failed to submit their assignments on time and were subsequently penalized. I appreciate that there may have been some good reasons for the lateness. But let me repeat why I penalize late assignments. I'm unable to establish the genuineness of excuses and unable to evaluate their relative merits. What concerns me more is that other students have similar problems but never complain or reveal their problems to me. If I give extra time for submission without penalty, then I am effectively penalizing the students who get their essays in on time. Previous experience with other classes has taught me that students who submit work on time get annoyed if they see colleagues getting away scot-free.

'I should also say to you that I have used the same system with other classes both here and at other universities. The pattern of student behaviour was similar to yours – no better, no worse. It seems to me that it is better to be fair to everyone, rather than to favour a few.

'However, if this class feels that I have been unfair then you must tell me, by majority vote or consensus, or whatever system feels best to you as Pacific Islanders. I will then take appropriate action to remove the penalty marks.

'The second point that I wish to make concerns my feeling that some of you seem highly displeased with your low marks for assignments and tutorial papers. I can understand students feeling disappointed with such marks. But the course work which attracted poor grades did not deserve any higher scoring. This is not to say that they can't be improved; I indicated on each student's paper the strengths and weaknesses, and how subsequent papers can be improved.

'I would not insult you by lowering the standards. The South Pacific has enough problems without imposing sub-standard degrees upon its students. I'm sure you want to leave university feeling proud of your achievements and with the knowledge that your degree will be acceptable in Australia, New Zealand, Britain, America, Canada, or anywhere else in the world. If this doesn't bother you, I can quite easily give you all As, but I don't think that's what you really want.

'That's all I have to say. Thank you for listening and for your attention. If you have any questions or comments, please feel free to make them. Or if you want to speak to me privately, either as individuals or in small groups, please see me in my office or at the tutorials'.

My comments took no longer than five minutes. The silence was deafening. Since there were no questions, I finished the class and told them I'd see them at the tutorials, since I had given out the tutorial paper the previous week.

Next day, and just before the first tutorial, one of the Fijians who had moaned greatly about his course work marks came to see me in my office (I had no set times for consultation and operated an open door policy, which was not the norm at the university). He remarked that he had been speaking to a large group of his class colleagues and he was here to represent their views. They offered me their apologies most sincerely, especially for their behaviour at the tutorials. They had not meant to cause me so much distress and so many problems. They had really enjoyed the class and appreciated that I was trying to set a high but fair standard and that it was up to them to achieve it. The student went on to say that on reflection they also felt that the penalty mark system was fairest to the great majority of students. He said that one of their problems was that some lecturers didn't worry about when they got essays in, but they agreed with what I had said the previous day about many people feeling annoyed when late assignments did not attract penalties.

It seemed to me that this was a very sincere apology in the traditional Island way and that the students were not just trying to keep in my good books for the sake of getting better grades. Thus I immediately accepted their apologies and asked the student to convey my acceptance to the class, which he did, as I was later told by another student. I said that it was only after a great deal of thought that I had made my comments but that I felt it was necessary to bring into the open the tensions existing between us.

The subsequent tutorials went quite well, although there was a bit of tension in the air. At the end of the second tutorial, the other Fijian who had expressed annoyance at her course work marks approached me. She said that she fully supported what the other student had told me, and she again apologized for the behaviour of the class. 'Those Western Samoans, they don't want to work. We'll all need to work hard, since we want to feel that the degree was earned, not given away'. I thanked her very much for her comments, which I found very supportive. We then chatted for a while about a question in the tutorial paper, one which she had found difficult.

For the rest of the semester I had no problems with the class, in either tutorials or lectures. Only one person failed to turn up for the class test, and he did not offer any excuse. Nevertheless, it would be wrong to suggest that rapport returned to the same level as it had been in the first half of the semester. The Fijian Indian female student was quite pleasant and worked away diligently. However, the Western Samoan student who had caused me all the aggravation rarely turned up to lectures or tutorials and his friends were not much better.

I marked the final exam blind, as is my usual practice, in order to avoid any bias. The Fijian students passed, but the Western Samoan student failed. As it turned out, the penalty marks did not greatly influence the final gradings. However, I made a point of getting the paper of the Western Samoan checked by a colleague, without giving the circumstances surrounding this request. My colleague scored the paper within 5 per cent of my mark.

I had not told the students that I was leaving the university, having put in my notice in mid-March, well before the problem blew up. However, they discovered in the last week of the semester that I was to depart in mid-July for a university in New Zealand. I was touched when some of them came to see me just before I left to wish me well and to thank me for my efforts on their behalf. As I flew out of Suva, I reflected on my experiences in the semester just completed, and particularly on the action I had taken. Did I get it right? Could I have done better? Should I make any changes in New Zealand?

- *How well do you think the teacher handled this incident?*
- *How far do you think the problems this teacher encountered were of his own making? What is the reasoning behind your response to this question?*
- *If faced with a similar incident, how would you have acted; what would you have done differently?*

PART THREE

Upon arriving in New Zealand, I did change my policy on course work. At the beginning of the first session in 1989, I informed my class of my normal policy but said that I wanted them to participate in deciding the fate of late assignments. I asked for four volunteers to form a small group, which would debate the issue and sound out the views of their classmates. Their decision was that any student who felt that he or she would have problems with submitting assignments on time would have to let the monitoring group know in advance so that the reason for lateness could be assessed. Assuming it was an acceptable excuse, no penalty would be imposed for an assignment handed in up to a week late. After that date, late assignments would attract a penalty of 10 per cent for each additional day late. The class was happy with this policy and I made it a course-work requirement. I also agreed that I would abide by their decisions.

In the 1990 session the class again accepted my proposal that they should decide the policy on late assignments. However, on this occasion the student group decided that a penalty should apply immediately after the submission date.

So far, 90 per cent of the assignments have been handed in on time and none has been more than four days late. There has been only one complaint, from a student who felt that it was unfair to penalize an assignment submitted one day late. However, he accepted the class decision and agreed that the class should decide such matters.

- *What are your thoughts on the new system that the lecturer has introduced? What are its main strengths in comparison with the previous system? Do you see any problems in the new system?*

Discussion

This case focuses on the contract between teacher and students concerning assignments, and what happens when assignments are handed in late. There is an obvious movement in the teacher's approach to such a contract from the beginning of the case to the end. The incidents which form the basis for the case obviously caused the teacher to think seriously about the way this contract with students was created, and to make changes to the way he approached this task.

At the beginning of the case we see the teacher spelling out what will happen to assignments which are handed in late. The students play no part in this and so could not be expected to have any 'ownership' of the system which the teacher outlines. It is imposed upon them, even though the imposition may have been, from the teacher's standpoint, for the best of reasons. We are given an outline of the thinking behind the teacher's treatment of late assignments, but it is not clear whether the students were given a similar rationale. All we know is that the students made no response in the first lecture to the conditions laid down by the teacher, and the teacher interprets this at the time as the students agreeing with his position and regarding it as fair.

Such an interpretation is problematic, however, for as we have seen in a number of cases, statements made at the beginning of a course, no matter how clearly articulated, are very often questioned only later on when the full consequences which flow from them become apparent or urgent. In the teacher's mind a contract may have been agreed, but the notion that a contract can be set and sealed for all time in the first class of the year is surely mistaken. Certainly a great deal of the contract between teacher and students can be negotiated early in the course, but this must be subject to later review and revision as the course progresses and as circumstances change. The very term 'contract' may be unhelpful in this regard, as the idea of a signed and sealed document is not a particularly helpful metaphor for what should be a continuing process of negotiation and accommodation.

It is good that the teacher has a clear and reasoned position on late assignments and that he makes this position clear at the very start of the course. This is certainly preferable to having to make up a policy after the event, or failing to apply systematic and constant criteria. However, it is perhaps worth examining a little more closely the teacher's reasons for taking his particular stance.

He claims that he cannot establish the validity of reasons for students wanting to hand work in late. By the end of the case study, of course, he has changed his position so far that he has found it possible to hand over this task to a small committee of students. The issue is not therefore that reasons for handing work in late *cannot* be vetted, but rather that the teacher *prefers not* to vet them. Most teachers would sympathize with this position but would still see the need to look at excuses as a necessary chore in order to avoid a greater injustice, for the position that *any* excuse is as valid (or invalid) as the next is surely not sustainable. Most departments or courses therefore have guidelines as to what is acceptable (production of a doctor's certificate, for example) and mechanisms or a forum for weighing cases. Most teachers, however, have grounds to suspect that unfair advantage is taken of these processes from time to time.

The teacher's next reason concerns the unfairness to those students who did hand work in on time if their errant peers are allowed to hand work in late. There are some problems with this argument, too, as it appears to rely on students not having a legitimate reason for wanting to hand an assignment in late. Few teachers would argue that students should be allowed to hand work in at any time and offer no explanation. Such a practice would be seen as causing unnecessary administrative problems by many teachers. However, if students have to establish legitimate grounds for handing their assignments in late, it is difficult to see how this disadvantages those students who did not experience similar difficulties. The argument that *everyone* has difficulties fails to take account of the differential weight of difficulties, and of the fact that they have to be legitimate and their validity established by the system in place.

Another reason given by the teacher for not allowing late submission is that students do not ask for final exams to be postponed. Again, however, this argument is difficult to sustain as there is usually a fairly elaborate set of rules to allow exceptions for those who fail to take exams. Rules vary among institutions and faculties, and their interpretation is the subject of keen debate almost every year. But there are usually mechanisms for considering extenuating circumstances for missing an examination, and students may be given another opportunity to take the exam or, should circumstances warrant, to be granted a pass without having taken the exam. This argument is thus not a particularly strong one.

The final reason for the policy of the teacher at the beginning of the case is that prompt submission of assignments means he can ensure prompt feedback. This is an excellent argument, and there is much evidence to suggest that the feedback students receive on their work soon after handing it in is the most effective. Students' interest in the assignment they have produced is at its peak when the assignment has just been completed, and the feedback they receive then or shortly after will be of much interest to them. Receiving back the assignment with comments a term, or even two terms, later has much less of an effect. In the meantime, students may have produced many more assignments for a variety of courses, and in some circumstances may barely be able to remember what the assignment was about. The teacher in this case study could have elaborated this point to the students and have carried it further in terms of the contract he negotiated with them. Thus he could have suggested that, as part of the contract, if they submitted their assignment on the due date, he would undertake to return the assignments, marked, and with full comments, by so many days later. When students pointed out that other teachers did not penalize them for handing assignments in late, he could also have pointed out that most teachers did not return assignments quickly, as he was committing himself to do. Such a move could have made the initial contract which the teacher suggested appear fairer by imposing conditions on *both* parties in comparison with the one-sided set of conditions which he announced.

It could therefore be argued that, to some extent, the problems the teacher encountered with the late assignments were of his own making, due to the fact that he unilaterally disallowed any form of extenuating factor from consideration. Students could thus legitimately feel aggrieved that, despite having the best of excuses due to matters quite outside of their control, these would not be taken into any account. The fact that the teacher (quite properly) had given them ample time in which to complete the assignment does not discount their resentment at this, as circumstances could have conspired late in the period to prevent their handing the assignment in on time. Having to attend a funeral was a case in point, and this also illustrates a possible tension between the cultural norms of the teacher and students. For the students, attendance at a funeral may not have been a matter of choice, and the funeral and associated activities may well have lasted a number of days. The teacher sought to banish all such considerations from his policy, but one wonders whether this really is possible, or whether it merely illustrates the power of one cultural tradition over another.

The teacher is to be commended for being attuned to the feeling of the class and for bravely confronting what he saw as the unfortunate gulf which had developed between himself and his students. We can imagine his nervousness in the days before he was to face the class and the nervous tension when he brought matters into the open. His speech was moderate and conciliatory, restating his own case but giving students the opportunity to produce a better system if they chose. This may be seen as seeking to involve them, to some extent, after the event, and again one might postulate that seeking a greater level of participation earlier in the course may have reduced the problems. The effect of the speech from the teacher's point of view was thus good. Despite the fact that the teacher and students still did not enter a dialogue to discuss their differences, the students were conciliatory and tried to restore their relationship with the teacher. The teacher's original policy therefore stood intact and the students accepted it, despite there being some serious questions as to its validity (as discussed above). This apart, the teacher and students appear to have parted on good terms.

The teacher's new policy, which he developed after reflecting on this experience, answers the basic problem of his former system. Specifically, the students participated fully in the formation of the new rules, and they could thus be seen to have allegiance to and 'ownership' of the new system. This was a positive move and one which the students appeared to value. On the other hand, one might ask whether the teacher has this time gone too far in seeking student involvement in the formation of the new policy, and, more specifically, its implementation. For example, one may ask whether a student would feel comfortable explaining a highly personal physical, emotional, family or other matter to a small group of his or her peers. One wonders too at the composition of the committee, how it was chosen and what kind of representation it could legitimately claim. Finally, was the teacher right to disclaim any right to a voice on the committee? He could quite rightly claim that his was the ultimate responsibility for the decisions made by the committee. Was he thus wise to deny himself any participation in the process by which decisions were made? For example, could he have suggested an appeal process which would have included either himself or one of his colleagues? These kinds of questions are precisely the type to be raised in his dialogue with students and to be refined as the 'contract' between the students and the teacher develops over time. At least with the new policy in place there is a greater feeling of confidence that difficulties which arise during the course may be brought into the open and discussed, and that the problems encountered under the old system are thus far less likely.

QUESTIONS FOR PERSONAL REFLECTION

- *Do you explicitly discuss what will happen to late assignments with your classes? How far are students asked to participate in this process?*
- *Do you have a 'contract' covering matters like the late submission of assignments? When is this made? Do you have any way of updating this contract, of reviewing and if needs be revising it?*
- *If you allow late submission for extenuating circumstances, how do you ensure the validity of these, how do you 'weigh' excuses? Have you ever considered that there may be different cultural interpretations of what constitutes a legitimate extenuating circumstance?*
- *Are there any other implications or lessons to be drawn from this case which have application in your own teaching? Is there anything in your own teaching practice that you need to reconsider after having read and reflected on this case?*

The Obesity Outburst

Case reporter: Peter Schwartz

Issues Raised

The main issue raised in this case is that of dealing with an outburst or challenge by a student in a traditional lecture setting. There is also an issue concerning the consequences of students' expectations when attending a large group session which departs from the normal lecture format.

Background

The incident described in the case occurred in the early 1980s. It took place near the start of a course in clinical biochemistry for medical students. The session on obesity was the fifth or sixth in the course. The male teacher was 40 years old, had an education in medicine and had been teaching for 14 years when the incident occurred. The students were mostly 20 or 21 years old, including the male student who interrupted the session.

PART ONE

I had been teaching clinical biochemistry to medical students for about ten years when this incident occurred. Certainly I'd had the occasional (though fortunately rare) problem with my classes, but this one has stayed clearest in my memory.

With a class of 120–200 students, no provision for small group work and little knowledge of educational principles, I found it difficult in my early years of teaching to avoid lecturing. None the less, even from the first I experimented with ideas that seemed, from my own experience as a student and from the reading I did, to be sensible. These included taking breaks in the middle of lectures, using self-quizzing at the ends of lectures and incorporating humorous, relevant quotations at intervals during the lectures. All of these went over well, as did my key decision to highlight topics of undoubted interest and relevance to the students, even though their explanations in biochemical terms might be much poorer than were those for other topics that were usually taught. Hence issues like diabetes, cancer, atherosclerosis – and obesity – featured among the topics I dealt with.

As I learned more about teaching and became more confident, I gradually moved away from straight lecturing. By the time of the 'obesity outburst', I had evolved a system whereby the basic factual material for my topics was available to the students in a series of printed units (including objectives, text, self-quiz and a guide to additional reading) so that the class sessions could be used differently. The students were aware of what the topic for each session would be and that I would not be giving straight lectures. They were advised not to attend if they expected only to get an ordinary lecture but that if they *did* intend to come along, they should have read the prescribed materials in advance.

The actual class sessions were used to let the students see the relevance of what they were learning and to apply the information. Hence I had short and long clinical problems for them to solve at some sessions, interviews with patients at others, and panel discussions with visitors at still others. I tried to keep the sessions as informal as possible and wanted to get the students as involved as I could. By always staying near the front row of seats in the large lecture room (never behind the lectern), by encouraging comments and questions and by being able to refer to each of the students in the class by name, I hoped to show my closeness to them and my concern for them even though faced with such a large group. This seemed to work well almost all the time – one of the exceptions is about to appear!

Whenever possible, I tried to engage the feelings of the students as well as their intellects, so, for example, in a session on diabetes we had a dramatic interview with a young patient who had gone rapidly blind at least in part through an arrogant act by her doctor's receptionist. I felt that a discussion of obesity lent itself to such considerations as well. I was well aware from my reading and from studies that I had heard of that obese people face a lot of negative attitudes from others, in the workplace and elsewhere. I wanted to build a consideration of this into the class on obesity. My session on the topic was divided into three sections: (1) a brief discussion of why we as doctors might be worried about obesity; (2) a summary of some of the latest ideas on what might go wrong biochemically so that obese people become that way without necessarily overeating; and (3) a consideration of one of the treatments for obesity, this one being a non-medical one that is at the same time sound and as effective as most of the methods offered by the medical profession. For this last, I invited two or three of the staff and clients of Weight Watchers to come along and describe their methods and then answer any questions from the students. They sat in the front row of the lecture room until I invited them to come up to some chairs facing the class for their part of the session.

At the time of the outburst, I had already run the session this way several times, so I was quite relaxed about it. As usual, I began by considering why we should worry about obesity. I highlighted the health problems associated with overweight but said that, really, except for people who are grossly overweight, the *medical* risks were not that great. I went on to say that I thought a greater problem was the *psychological* one, the result of prejudice and advertising.

To bring this home and to personalize it, I described my own feelings, saying that I feel this way although I can't account for why I do. I said that I am repelled by obese people and find them particularly unattractive. I indicated that hidden in there is what is probably a 'moral judgement': I keep having the feeling that obese people are just gluttonous and deserve what they get. I pointed out that of course I'm well aware that many or even most obese people *don't* actually overeat but that if I can feel and react this way while knowing the facts, what can we expect of others who don't know this?

At this point, one of the students midway up the lecture room loudly and angrily interrupted: 'Wait a minute. I didn't come here to listen to your prejudices about obesity ...' That brought the class to a screeching halt. I don't recall whether the student went any further – that was far enough already to shatter my impression that this class would go as smoothly as had its similarly-run counterparts in previous years. Even if I were to continue the class as I had planned, this needed a response. But what sort of response? What do I do now?

- *What do you think the teacher did do next?*
- *What would you have done if you had been in his place?*

PART TWO

I must admit that the first thought that flashed through my mind when the student interrupted was to retort: 'You didn't have to come here *at all*', to give a reminder that I had no intention of giving straight lectures, and to reiterate that people shouldn't attend if they weren't prepared to do something different at the sessions.

Although I probably would have resisted the temptation to say that anyway, I was saved from doing so when another student near the front of the class turned around and told the one who interrupted that others *did* want to hear what I had to say. This plus the murmur of assent that followed it was enough to cool things down (and me in particular). Instead of a hostile reaction, I calmly explained that I was trying to give a point of view that I thought was widespread in the population and that it was not just my own. In addition, I wanted to show that if I could feel that way *in spite of* knowing the scientific facts, think of how hard it would be to influence the opinions of others who didn't know what I knew.

The rest of the session went as smoothly as usual, and in fact I made use of the possible extra embarrassment of having the outburst occur in front of visitors by asking the people from Weight Watchers about whether my feelings about obese people were widespread and what influence such feelings had on the people who attended Weight Watchers.

I thought long and hard after the session and decided to take one further measure to minimize any antagonism in the class. At the start of my next session (on a different topic) I apologized if I had offended anyone and tried to make it clear that I wasn't trying to indoctrinate them or suggest that my way of thinking was appropriate (and acknowledged, in fact, that it was wrong) but that I was just describing it truthfully and as being representative of a widespread attitude, the effects of which were probably more significant in obesity than the health risks.

- *How well do you think the teacher handled this incident? What other options were open to him and what might have been the consequences of taking them?*
- *How would you have acted if faced with this situation? Would you have raised the issue again in the next class as this teacher did?*

Discussion

On the face of it, the issue in this case is disruptions to classes (particularly lectures) and how to deal with them. However, underlying this are several factors which may be considered. Among the most important of these are the educational contract between teachers and students and their expectations of class sessions. In this case, the teacher had one view of the role of lectures in his course. He had questions concerning their value for learning, had tried to improve them, and had then abandoned traditional lecturing entirely. By the time of the incident, he used 'lecture' sessions to motivate students and to let them see the meaning of the material they were expected to have studied on their own before the class sessions. Still, he controlled the proceedings and appeared to believe that all students would accept his notion of what the learning environment was to be. He also believed that students would be interested in his own feelings, and he attempted to engage their emotions as well as their intellects.

If the teacher was attempting to redefine the lecture as more student-centred and emotionally engaging and less directed and controlled by the teacher, then there appears to be some distance between his espoused aims and his actual behaviour. His immediate emotion when the outburst came was one of anger. This may have been for any of a number of reasons to do with: reacting to a threat to his authority; embarrassment in front of visitors; disruption to his plans and his version of the teaching/learning contract. In short, his initial reaction may have been less sympathetic to students and their views than we might have expected. While claiming to want the students to think, to be involved and to acknowledge feelings, his first reaction is annoyance when a student *does* express himself. Had the teacher wanted students to be involved, he might have had *them* express their opinions or identify what *they* thought the general perception of obese people was. On the other hand, the students may have been reluctant to disclose their own feelings had the teacher not already made a similar disclosure.

The student who interjected was quite brave to do so in a large class and in such a fashion. He obviously must have felt strongly about what was going on. However, we do not know whether it was a reaction to what the teacher was saying (as suggested by the content of the interjection) or at least partly a result of frustration caused by a perception that the teacher was failing to 'deliver the goods' and instead was airing his own prejudices.

If the teacher *had* replied angrily, it may have been that his sincerity and enthusiasm could have reduced the negative effects of such a response. But the fortunate reaction by another student and the subsequent mild response by the teacher probably worked to the teacher's advantage by minimizing hostility from the other students. Even though they might not have appreciated the outburst, they could well have sympathized with a classmate subjected to an angry and personal comment from the teacher. Had the others imagined themselves in a similarly vulnerable position, they may have responded antagonistically and the atmosphere of the class could have been soured for some time afterward.

Once the interruption had occurred, what were some other options open to the teacher and what might their consequences have been? He could have ignored the interruption, although there would not appear to be a good reason for doing so, especially as the incident could hardly be dismissed as of no consequence. In addition, the teacher seems not to be the type to ignore such a clear sign that something important was happening in his class. He could have tried to engage the student in dialogue. This might have led to a heated exchange and certainly would have caused more disruption to the class. On the other hand, if the student's outburst had simply been due to a misunderstanding or misinterpretation of the teacher's remarks, then the situation may have been clarified. In a similar vein, the teacher might have tried harder to incorporate the student's reaction into the class: a course of action which he actually did attempt by trying to justify his own comments and extending discussion to the visitors. As is usually the situation, anything more substantial would have required some very fast thinking and alteration to the teacher's plans.

What can be taken from this case is the importance of teachers being constantly alert to the possibility of explosive situations suddenly arising in class. Should such an occasion arise, teachers need to be aware of the danger of making a hasty remark which could destroy the good work they have previously put into building rapport with their students.

It is probably wise for teachers to weigh very carefully the possible consequences of revealing their attitudes about controversial issues. (A similar point could also be made with regard to the use of humour.) While such revelations may enrich the discussion and allow students to get a better impression of the teacher's personality, they also have the potential to offend and to antagonize some students. Should this happen, the teacher needs to have put a lot of work into making students believe that their thoughts and feelings, irrespective of whether they are shared by the teacher, are welcome in class. If their views will be accepted and carefully weighed and considered in a tolerant class atmosphere, students may be more inclined to produce thoughtful and tolerant articulations of their feelings and thoughts, rather than intolerant outbursts.

QUESTIONS FOR PERSONAL REFLECTION

- *Are there any aspects of either the form or content of any of your classes which you might consider in attempting to minimize the chance of an explosive situation developing (assuming that you wish to avoid it)?*
- *Is there any way in which you can prepare yourself to deal quickly with an outburst in class to minimize the damage it might do to the atmosphere of the class and your rapport with students?*
- *Is it possible that there could be a difference in perception between yourself and your students about the purposes of your teaching sessions? How could you find out and, if there were a difference, what would you do?*
- *Even though you may consider it to be desirable, do you feel that you can deal safely and comfortably with attitudes as well as knowledge while working with a large group? Are there any precautions you could take?*
- *Are there any other implications of this case which you might want to consider for your own teaching practice?*

A Case of Credibility

Case reporter: The person who reported this case wishes to remain anonymous

---

Issues Raised

The central action in this case concerns a challenge to a teacher as he is delivering a lecture in which his own material and that of the textbook are at variance. This raises the issue of how far students should be spoonfed a non-contentious account of knowledge and how far they should have to struggle for their own understandings. Tied up in this is also the nature of the assessment regime and the perceptions of the teacher and students as to what the purpose of the course was.

Background

This case study involves events which took place in a university Faculty of Physical Education in 1980. The teacher was male, 35 years old, and had several years of experience teaching chemistry, mathematics and physics in high schools before undertaking postgraduate study. He was now in the first year of a university appointment but had some teaching experience as a teaching assistant while a doctoral student. He had not previously had sole responsibility for a course at university.

PART ONE

Background to the incident

On taking up my university appointment, I was dismayed to find that, although the subject which I was to teach had been taught for several years, there were no teaching material resources. Fortunately, I was familiar with the textbook, but I did have to work hard to prepare the subject outline and a complete set of lecture notes in a short period of time.

The subject I was teaching was Introductory Biomechanics and this was part of the required first-year course in the Department of Human Movement Studies. The university scheduled teaching in two 13-week semesters. There were two one-hour lectures scheduled each week and a number of laboratory/tutorial sessions organized by the lecturer but taught by a tutor. The subject was open to first-year science and physiotherapy students so that, of the 150 students enrolled, approximately 100 would be Human Movement Studies students. Limited entry to the course meant that the students were of high ability but with quite varying backgrounds. Many had not taken advanced mathematics or physics at secondary school; this was a disadvantage in the mathematically oriented subject being taught.

In the subject prescription I had clearly set out what I planned to cover and how the material was to be evaluated. I tended to give traditional-style lectures but I had commented that the material in the lectures was supplementary to the material in what I considered to be an excellent text. Cumulative assessment was to be used. I had some notions about what I wanted to achieve in my teaching and had stated early in the class that 50 per cent was not perceived as a pass. I said that being incorrect half the time was not acceptable (these notions were considered unusual at the time). Written laboratory reports were graded weekly and mid-semester and final examinations, approximately 30 per cent multiple-choice, were also given. On the multiple-choice questions, two marks were given for a correct response while one mark was deducted for an incorrect response. The students appeared to be quite happy with the subject structure and assessment procedures. At least, no objections had been forthcoming and the semester seemed to be progressing as I had anticipated. The students appeared to be taking their work seriously and had made a good start to the semester.

The incident

My recollection is that the incident occurred sometime soon after mid-semester. I was in the middle of a lecture and had reached a point where my lecture material was different from the presentation of the topic in the text. I had, I thought, finished explaining why the difference existed and had paused, inviting comment, before going on to the next topic. The outburst was from the centre of the lecture room: 'What are we supposed to believe then if we can't believe the textbook?' This comment surprised me and my response was a question to the students as a body: 'Do you believe everything you read?' There was now clearly a general stirring, a rumble of discontent and a quick reply: 'Should we believe everything we hear in lectures?' I took the position that they should not accept without question things that they read or were told. Lecture material should be supplemented with material from readings and notes from the text. There may be disagreements on some of the issues. In these cases it is important to work out why different points of view are presented.

The students expressed the reservation that they did not have the competence in the subject to be able to make their own judgements. The discussion continued in this vein for about 20 minutes, until the end of the lecture time. What do I do now?

- *How would you have handled the initial question? What would you have said?*
- *Would you have done anything after the lecture?*
- *What do you think the teacher actually did next?*

PART TWO

I left the lecture room feeling satisfied with the outcome of the blow-up but relieved that my neck was still intact and resolving not to fall into the same trap again!

I had the feeling that the students were having difficulty with the subject and wanted me to present only material that was black and white. In the remainder of the lectures for this class I presented less challenging material, perhaps subconsciously to avoid conflict! In retrospect I feel that I was being pressured to keep to the straight and narrow and not to deviate too much from the text and the way things were normally done. I also arranged for personal tutorial sessions for an invited group of students selected on the basis of poor results on the mid-semester examination.

The next time I taught the subject I de-emphasized the grading aspect. The deduction of points for incorrect responses proved an unpopular grading procedure and was dropped. A standard for a pass was still stated to be about 75 per cent in overall assessment.

- *How well do you think the teacher responded to this incident?*
- *If faced with a similar incident, how would you have acted; what would you have done differently?*

Discussion

As with many of the events reported in this book, the actual incident may be no more than the tip of the iceberg. In this case study there seem to be a number of concerns regarding the purpose and operation of the course over which the teacher and students may have held differing positions. This is confounded by a diverse student body which itself is heterogeneous in needs and wants. For example, there are a large number of students for whom the course is necessary, foundational to their studies and presumably of intrinsic interest. However, within this Human Movement group and among other students, as for example those from physiotherapy, there may be students who regard it as a peripheral yet compulsory chore. Still others, for example those from science who are taking the course by choice, may have a strong intrinsic interest in the area, or on the other hand may see it as an easy option. We can only guess at what the various motivations to take the course may be. However, each group brings with it a differing level of knowledge and preparation for the course, in addition to their interest and motivation. This is most apparent in the area of mathematics and physics, where the teacher reports that many of the students have a poor background despite the fact that he sees these areas as central to the subject he is teaching.

The lecturer is therefore facing a difficult task from the beginning in that he is trying to cater for differing groups within the class, each pursuing the subject from a differing perspective, seeking to get differing things out of the course, and starting from differing knowledge bases. Satisfying such diverse demands is a challenge which many teachers face, and which they can work on by seeking student feedback, by constantly monitoring the course and adapting it to maintain a satisfactory balance. However, the teacher in this case study is in his first year of teaching the course, he has no material resources to fall back on and he appears to be uncomfortably alone in deciding what he will do. In pitching the level of his lectures, he appears to be trying to extend the students by going further than the textbook ('supplementing' is the word he uses) and challenging some of its materials or positions. Perhaps we may see here a difference in the position of a new lecturer, seemingly fresh from research and keen to challenge and stimulate, and his *first*-year students, nervous of their ability to cope, especially as many of them have a poor background in subjects upon which the course apparently relies heavily. Given these circumstances, teachers would usually be prudent to go slowly and build confidence in their students before seeking to stretch them further.

What actually causes the incident itself is a little unclear. According to the teacher, he has just explained the difference between his interpretation and that of the textbook. At least some of the students feel that he has not done this adequately. However, when they ask whether they are to believe the textbook or the teacher, he answers that they have to work out how different points of view come about. This is confusing in that it was exactly this point that the teacher was supposed to have clarified and explained before being challenged. Instead of going back over the ground he claims to have covered, however, he suggests that it is for the students to work out for themselves. They then say they do not have the competence to do so, and with this we can enter a perennial educational paradox.

The problem here is that teachers know that much 'real' learning can come only when students grapple with and find their own constructions, understandings and interpretations of materials and concepts with which they are unfamiliar. Students know that this can be frustrating, inefficient and beyond their competence. The perennial paradox lies in the fact that both may well be right. The only way through this is to consider the circumstances and purposes of a particular situation in order to gauge how far apart the two positions really are. In the present case, however, the paradox appears to be in the perception of the teacher rather than apparent in the issue. This is a first-year course being taken by varying types of students, many with a poor background in subjects which are considered essential to the course. As such, one has sympathy for the students' demands for 'straightforward', 'black and white' or unproblematic 'instruction'. And this is in fact what the teacher decides to give them after the challenge, albeit somewhat sheepishly. In other words, the teacher is feeling his way as a newcomer to teaching the course, coming as he is from recent research work, and is discovering that for these particular circumstances he must be circumspect in pitching the course at a level which is intelligible to the students. This is not to say that he cannot introduce more problematic or contradictory materials or interpretations in the course, but it does suggest that in these circumstances he will need to do so sparingly and very carefully. The students clearly did not feel confident enough to value the 'supplementary' nature of the lecture material and obviously thought that they were being asked to 'run before they could walk'. The teacher, too, appears to accept this by the end of the case.

This latter point may also be of interest with respect to the role of assessment in the case. In contrast to the teacher's espoused position of giving 'supplementary' lectures and alternative interpretations to the textbook, the assessment regime appears to be of a pretty 'black and white' nature. It seems the teacher is using a 'mastery' type assessment system, where students are required to show a high level of mastery of the course content (75 per cent in fact) before they can pass. This kind of approach is supposedly favoured where 'uncontroversial' material is concerned, where interpretation, ambiguity and shades of meaning are not considered to be of importance, and often where testing by multiple-choice items is sufficient to demonstrate competence. It could thus be argued that the teacher is giving the impression through his assessment system that he is looking for exactly the 'factual' or 'black and white' approach to subject knowledge that the students request in his lecture.

Finally, the question could be asked whether the teacher acted too defensively with respect to the incident which took place in the lecture. As we have seen, one interpretation of the case would suggest that, given the circumstances, the students had a legitimate point in asking the questions they did. However, the lecturer seems to have been on the defensive from the start and to have taken this questioning personally, as a threat to his own credibility. The title of the case study is interesting in this regard, as is his relief at getting out with his 'neck intact'. He vows not to get into such a situation again, but if by this he means *students* asking questions which have profound importance for them, then this is surely a pity. Most of us who are teachers, especially at the start of our careers, feel extremely vulnerable to attack in the public forum of the lecture room. Our egos and personalities are intricately entwined with our subject knowledge and our performance as a teacher. An innocuous question from a student on subject matter can thus quickly be interpreted as a personal attack on the teacher as a person. Encouraging *truly* open discussion in class, being able to separate our egos from the process of the class, and not taking criticism personally, are skills which are acquired slowly and probably never fully learned.

QUESTIONS FOR PERSONAL REFLECTION

- *Do you have mixed groups of students who are looking to obtain different things from your courses? How do you balance the needs of these varying groups?*
- *What is your position on balancing the need to give students the confidence to be able to achieve on your courses against an antipathy to 'spoon feeding'? Have you ever got the balance wrong? If so, how and why?*
- *How far does the assessment regime in your courses reflect the differing levels of*

students you teach? Do you run fundamentally different types of assessment for junior students and for senior students? Should you?

- *The title of this case study and the reaction of the teacher during the incident suggest that he was defensive and took fairly personally what could be interpreted as a legitimate question in class. Do you react similarly? How could you change this behaviour if you wished to do so?*
- *Are there any other implications or lessons to be drawn from this case which have application in your own teaching? Is there anything in your own teaching practice that you need to reconsider after having read and reflected on this case?*

The Median Marks Issue

Case reporter: Pauline A Mahalski

Issues Raised

The issues raised in this case are focused on the rights of teachers to produce their own assessment or teaching practices and the rights of colleagues to question these. Notions of academic freedom and collegiality are thus brought into the argument. The differing purposes of assessment are discussed and the wider (political) implications of assessment are touched on. The issue of maintaining good collegial relationships despite disagreements on matters of work is also raised.

Background

The year-long Environmental Psychology course at the centre of this case comprised lectures, tutorials, seminars and projects. It was in the mid-1970s that the incidents described in the case occurred, and they began about one-third of the way through the course. The teacher who took the stance opposing Ken was female and both she and Ken were about 40 years old at the time.

PART ONE

It all happened a long time ago, so the details are getting rather dim, but the whole business aroused so much emotion at the time that those of us who were involved will never forget the incident entirely. It was probably during one of the departmental tea breaks that I first heard one of my colleagues say: 'Have you heard about Ken's agreement with his third-year class in Environmental Psychology?' I said that I had not.

'Well, he and the class have agreed that, at the end of the course, all of the students will receive the median assessment mark of the whole class.'

'What on earth for?'

'Well, Ken and his class were discussing the harm which competition can do to society and lamenting the fact that even students miss chances to work cooperatively for the benefit of all.'

'And so they all will get the same mark! But that's a crazy idea! I don't think that competition is necessarily bad. One consequence of this could be that none of the class put in much work for the course at all. It's a distortion! Why did the class agree to the idea?'

'I don't know, but you know how persuasive Ken can be. Not all of the class agreed, but the majority did.'

'What do you think about it?'

'The class has agreed to it in a democratic way. They took a vote. We enjoy academic freedom at this university, so I agree that it is up to Ken and his class.'

'That seems to be taking academic freedom a bit far!'

Later, in idle moments, I gave more thought to the median marks scheme. How bland life would be without competition. Most people enjoy the chance to compete in some way, from time to time. Was it not absurd to label all competition 'bad'? Wasn't it all right for little old ladies to compete for the best plum jam at the Agricultural and Pastoral show? The more I thought about Ken and his median marks scheme, the more I thought that it was a bad idea. I resolved to discuss the matter with Ken and to present a range of counter-arguments, including the one that giving all the class the median mark was ignoring the underlying differences between the students and did not do justice to the students.

Perhaps this is the time to say something about my background and Ken's. We were both about the same age, and although I had been in the department for a few years longer, he was senior in status to me. I had come to psychology rather late and via a British background, whereas Ken had an almost unbroken and distinguished career in psychology, via an American background. Ken was very bright. He had acquired his PhD with a prestigious supervisor, and he had received top rankings as a teacher at an American university. He had published several articles on verbal learning and perceptual illusions and he had written a workbook to accompany one of the best texts in introductory psychology. Before he accepted his position at the university, he had worked for several years on the comprehension of instruction in a human factors research laboratory. While working there he maintained his interest in teaching by being active on a number of educational boards and writing about educational issues.

People often asked why Ken forsook his native land to come to the relatively quiet backwater of New Zealand. The answer, as one of his American friends put it, was that 'Ken had experienced a religious conversion without the benefit of God'. Ken's version of events was that, while he enjoyed the stimulus of the sharp minds of his American colleagues, he found himself increasingly disillusioned with the productivity, consumerism, materialism and technology games which characterized US society. A growing commitment to humanism, socialism, anti-war attitudes and environmental issues provoked him to seek a new life in New Zealand.

Soon after Ken arrived he initiated a major review of our curricula and teaching methods. He began to offer courses in human factors and environmental psychology, where the results of teaching and research could be readily applied. He also revolutionized his own lifestyle, adopting a low-technology, ecologically-conscious way of living. His marriage broke up and he sought the company of much younger people. In retrospect, he admitted that he had outraged his peer group and had enjoyed a belated adolescence.

I had my talk with Ken and got nowhere. My arguments had no appeal to him, as he rejected every one of them. In spite of his eloquence, I was equally unmoved by his arguments. It was a stalemate. The only thing to come out of it was an agreement that I be allowed to address his third-year class and put forward my arguments in favour of marking the class in the conventional way.

I did this several days later. There were about 20 students in the Environmental Psychology class. Many of the students were familiar to me, as I was teaching some of them in my own third-year class. The students listened patiently. I don't remember any discussion, just a few closing remarks from Ken which suggested to me that he had heard things which I had not said. I began to have very negative feelings about Ken. As I am normally a very unemotional person, the depths of these feelings surprised me.

The issue of the median marks was widely discussed among the staff of the Psychology Department and among the third-year students. The head of department was not prepared to take sides on the issue, as he said that the matter of the marks was up to Ken and his class. In any case, the head hated disputes and did all that he could to avoid them.

I discussed the issue briefly with one of the students who was in both Ken's class and my own. After we had finished discussing something to do with my course, she thanked me for getting involved with the median marks issue. She said that she had been against it all along but that it was difficult to go against the crowd. We did not resolve anything; we just commiserated with one another. I still felt that the normal assessment practice should be followed and that the idea of median marks should be dropped. What should I do now?

- *What do you think she did next?*
- *What, if anything, would you have done at this point?*

PART TWO

In the event, the issue was resolved without my having to take any further part in it. It was a source of some disquiet to Ken and his supporters, and to those who wished to stay out of the dispute, that it was the brightest and best of the third-year students who were most bitterly opposed to the median marks scheme. As these students were in the minority, their opposition to Ken and to their colleagues had cost them sleepless nights. Many of the staff also felt a strain from being on opposite sides of the dispute.

One reason that the best students objected to the scheme was that they were hoping to get scholarships which involved competition across the entire university campus. Obviously, a lower-than-deserved mark could compromise their chances. In the end it was some of these students who initiated actions which dragged Ken and the Environmental Psychology class back into the conventional fold.

Two of the brightest students went to see the dean of the Faculty of Arts. They told him their story and begged him to intervene. He did. In no time at all an edict was handed down from on high that this policy of awarding all members of a class the median mark of the class contravened university policy. Ken had to mark by conventional means.

Ken was not pleased and neither was the head of department, but the students who had complained and others of like mind uttered sighs of relief. I was glad that the matter had ended without any further intervention from myself and in accordance with my principles. But I cannot say that the matter really ended there. It took a long time for my negative feelings towards Ken to dissipate. I guess that others on different sides of the issue had similar problems. I found that I felt awkward dealing with Ken for a long time afterwards. However, given time, almost anything is possible, and eventually we were able to be friends again and re-establish warm, collegial relations.

- *With whom do you have the most sympathy – Ken or the female staff member who opposed him?*
- *How do you feel about the parts played in this incident by the female member of staff, the head of department and the dean of faculty?*

Discussion

This case touches on some fundamental issues concerning the purpose of assessment and the responsibilities of teachers to students and to their colleagues. It also raises issues concerning two of the higher education teacher's most sacred of cows: academic freedom and collegiality. There may be a wide range of interpretation of the case and it needs to be stressed that what follows is but one of the many which are possible.

The initial reaction of many teachers to this case may well be that, according to the doctrine of academic freedom, Ken was perfectly free to teach how he liked, and the female teacher who opposed Ken (let us call her Judy) had no right to intervene: it was none of her business. This argument could also cite the democratically taken decision within Ken's class and thus the support Ken had among the students for his approach to assessment. Such an argument would be difficult to maintain, however, as academic freedom never works in isolation from a context, and the notion that Ken's class could decide whatever it wanted with regard to assessment, or anything else, is simply not true. The context within which academic freedom works is largely that defined by the equally illusive notion of collegiality. What is acceptable is very often determined by what one's colleagues will accept, and the fact that they will usually accept quite a lot should not be taken to mean that there are no limits to what an individual teacher can do. Collegiality also suggests that Judy had a legitimate interest in the teaching practices of her colleague and the steps she took to discuss and debate the matter with him were well within the tradition of open discourse which a university is supposed to foster and encourage. Simply saying that it was none of Judy's business, therefore, will not do.

That having been said, we may next consider the cases put forward by Ken and by Judy. Here there is surprisingly little to go on. We see that Ken wishes to encourage cooperation among his students, and Judy seems to think Ken considers that *all* competition is bad. Both of these statements are problematic, however, as we do not know whether Ken really thinks all competition is bad, or if he simply sees setting student against student for a limited number of grades as contrary to the atmosphere of cooperation which he wants to encourage in his class. However, if this is the case, how will giving all students the median grade for the class encourage cooperation? And why the median grade? Why not announce at the beginning that all students would receive an A grade, as this could put them in exactly the right frame of mind to cooperate well with each other for the rest of the course? If Ken really wants to encourage students to cooperate, then sharing the grade that they obtain either as a whole class or as members of sub-groups is a sensible strategy. Making this both the same grade for the whole class and the median seems arbitrary and unnecessary.

On the other hand, Ken does recognize the political connotations associated with grading, whereas Judy seems quite oblivious to them. Ken's purpose is presumably to 'level' and to 'share' a common outcome and this is apparently in tune with his political philosophy. Judy's purpose appears to be to reward students' 'innate abilities', to do 'justice' to them, not to 'ignore the underlying differences' between them and to safeguard the place of competition without which 'it could be that none of the class would put in much work at all'. This is a classically conservative stance, where ability tends to be innate (society and education can effect little change), there is a pessimistic view of human nature (people must be pitted against each other and made to work) and it is only fair and just that the 'brightest' be allowed to shine. To this, Ken would presumably point out that there is little justice in a system which has already filtered out most of the disadvantaged by class, gender and race. The illusion of justice is maintained only by supporting the freedom of those individuals who get the most from the system. Justice for the majority is denied, their only freedom being to engage in the sacred competition which they are doomed to lose from the start. Ken's philosophy and assessment policy are explicitly linked and, on the face of it, complementary.

Judy does not see her alternative to Ken's system as being political, however, and refers to it simply as the 'conventional' approach. But what is this? Given the period of the case study (and also the subject area involved) it is probable that assessment would be graded on a normal curve. If this was indeed the case, then *this* procedure to many nowadays would seem as illogical and politically motivated as Ken's does to Judy. Giving a predetermined number of grades in each category, year after year, failing or brilliantly passing students not on what they can or cannot do, but on their performance relative to a small number of their peers, would seem perverse to many. Other alternatives to what Judy considers the 'conventional' approach would include mastery learning and assessment (where the vast majority could be expected to pass with a similar grade), self-assessment and peer-assessment. The latter two approaches have again, quite explicitly, been linked with the movement to empower students and encourage them to have greater autonomy in their own learning.

At the end of the day there are two major purposes which grading has served. First, it has been used to judge students according to each other, often using the apparatus of psychological testing and the normal distribution. Having judged students relative to each other (group-based assessment), the resources of everything from the educational system to society at large have been made available to the 'most deserving', that is, those who score highest. Second, assessment has been used to gauge what students actually know, usually with the view to aiding their learning (criterion-based assessment). The first function is mainly distributional while the second is educational. It seems that neither Judy nor Ken has placed much emphasis upon the *educational* function of assessment, and this is regrettable.

As to the actual incident, the final decision is difficult to interpret as we have no information to explain the dean's statement that Ken's grading is 'against university policy'. What *is* university policy, why, how can it be defended, should it be challenged or changed? None of this is revealed or even commented upon. Judy then leaves us with the impression that everyone is relieved by the outcome, whereas presumably the majority of Ken's class, along with Ken, would be very much less than pleased. By the end of the case, Ken and Judy are on reasonably good terms again, but we are still left with the impression that the whole episode has been traumatic for those involved. There is an issue here concerning how colleagues can disagree with each other and yet still maintain a good personal relationship. With regard to this, perhaps we can still learn something from the traditional conditions of collegiality, where colleagues had the opportunity to interact regularly, positively and in other than strict work situations. Perhaps, too, the head of department could have played a more dynamic role in facilitating the personal interactions of his colleagues in the case described.

QUESTIONS FOR PERSONAL REFLECTION

- *Have you ever considered the wider implications of the way you grade or mark assignments as outlined in this case? What is your position on the 'distributional' versus 'educational' purpose of assessment? Does this affect your assessment practice?*
- *Do you ever ask students to participate in discussing issues of grading and assessment?*
- *What is your understanding of the concept of academic freedom with respect to*

teaching practices? Do you believe that other teachers have the right to question your own assessment or other teaching practices?

- *Do you place any importance on the notion of collegiality? Do you or your department take any active steps to ensure and build good collegial relationships?*
- *Are there any other implications or lessons to be drawn from this case which have application in your own teaching? Is there anything in your own teaching practice that you need to reconsider after having read and reflected on this case?*

Tokenism

Case reporter: The person who reported this case wishes to remain anonymous

---

Issues Raised

A number of issues are raised by this case, including the appropriateness of a man teaching a course on feminist legal theory and whether or not the course should be compulsory. The importance of discussion for the course and the difficulties associated with encouraging discussion with a large class in a traditional lecture setting are also considered.

Background

The events of this case occurred in a large, compulsory third-year class in Legal Theory. The events began in the first week of the third term of the 1990 teaching year and continued through the term. The teacher was 34 years old. While this was his first year teaching the course involved, he had about two years of other teaching experience at tertiary level and had done considerable *ad hoc* teaching in a variety of settings, including universities, teachers' colleges, hospitals and conferences. The students were in their early 20s.

PART ONE

The course

The course was a general one in Legal Theory, a subject which has a scope that is open to substantial debate. It may include consideration of the relationships between law and related disciplines, such as ethics, social science, politics, religion or economics.

The lecturer, Ted, had an interest in issues concerning law and gender, and he had been reading in the expanding field of feminist legal theory. He was aware that a Women in Law association had been formed by students, and several senior women students were working in the gender area at Honours research level. He suspected that there would be a substantial demand among women students for a course in feminist legal theory.

This was the lecturer's first year on the faculty. On arrival he found that no course about law and gender issues was offered. Such courses are common in other law schools, the courses often being entitled 'Women and the Law'. These courses are attended mainly by women students and they are usually taught by women. The lecturer learned that a proposal had been made to the Faculty the previous year for such a course to be offered and this had been accepted by the staff in principle. However, no staff member had come forward to teach the course, so it had not gone ahead.

Faced with deciding what to teach in the second half year of the Legal Theory course, Ted decided to offer a course called 'Feminist Legal Theory'. It was to consist of 12 lectures and a series of readings. The readings were mainly contemporary writings by female legal theorists and they would be applied to problems of local legal doctrine, such as discrimination law, pay equity legislation and rape law reform.

The class

The class comprised 170 students. Approximately half the students were men, half women. Lectures were given in a large, tiered room, which seemed to discourage debate. Students at the back could not hear what students at the front had to say, requiring questions from students to be repeated by the lecturer. No tutorials were conducted, nor would resources permit them.

At the first of the 12 classes, Ted introduced the subject matter and then addressed the issue of whether it was appropriate for a man to teach such a course. As the preferred methodology of feminist legal theory is to approach the law from the standpoint of women's experiences, Ted conceded that a male teacher was not ideal, nor was the large class an ideal forum. He considered, however, that students should be exposed to feminist legal theory, that a general course on legal theory was an appropriate forum in which to discuss it, and that the likely alternative was that most students would not be exposed to it at all. He argued that feminist legal theory was aimed at both men and women. He informed the class that the idea of a Women in Law class had been accepted in principle by the Faculty but that no one had yet come forward to teach it.

He then asked the students if they believed that there was a distinct women's experience of law. In particular, he asked if there was a distinct women's experience of law *school*. He had set as readings for the first class two short pieces by women legal academics on the marginalization of women's concerns in law school curricula.

One forceful student then spoke out. She asked whether he really expected women students to answer such a question there and then when they had never been consulted on this before. The course was 'tokenist' and 'inappropriate'. Ted was portrayed as a sop sent to placate the students for the Faculty's failure to offer the Women in Law course. Ted agreed that the situation was not ideal and asked the woman if she would prefer it if the course was not offered. She said, 'Yes'. At this point several other women joined the debate, expressing approval of the course and the wish that it should continue. A male student said that he had no previous exposure to feminist thought but that he would welcome the opportunity.

After the class, Ted was approached by some of the women students. What did he mean that a Women in Law course had been accepted in principle but not offered? This was the worst type of tokenism. Why had a woman not been found to teach the course, by hiring someone specially if necessary? With such disagreement about the class at the first session, what should Ted do now?

- *What do you think Ted did next?*
- *What would you have done at this point?*

PART TWO

Ted informed the students who approached him after the first class that he would speak to women members of the faculty and try to ensure that the Women in Law course was offered the following year. He suggested to the students that they should themselves take their concerns to other faculty members, in particular those involved in the Staff Women's Caucus. Ted spoke to several women faculty members and to the dean. None of the women leaped forward to offer the course. The dean indicated that, with several staff on leave the following year, it was unlikely that any new courses would be offered.

At the next class, Ted told the students that he accepted that the subject matter was inappropriately handled by lecturing, but that the forum seemed to hinder free discussion. He proposed to give short lectures, half an hour at most, and then to open things for free discussion in the remaining 20 minutes. He stuck to this format through the remaining lectures. Wide discussion occurred after the presentations.

Ted took steps to try to ensure that a tutorial programme would be offered the following year. He proposed this at a staff meeting. The idea was accepted 'in principle', subject to the availability of resources. Some staff questioned the allocation of more resources to the course and whether it should remain compulsory. Ted agreed to formulate a questionnaire which would ask third-year students how they would like to see resources allocated. They were to be asked to choose among several options for the following year, such as tutorials being offered in subjects other than Legal Theory, or cutting large second-year classes into two streams. He circulated a draft of the questionnaire to all staff for comment and incorporated their suggestions. He then administered it to the class. The results confirmed that third-year students favoured the allocation of resources to tutorials in Legal Theory above all other options. He continued to lobby for this proposal.

At the conclusion of Ted's section of the course, 150 students (88 per cent of the class) completed an evaluation of the course. Students were asked to answer 21 rating-type questions and three open-ended questions which asked them to describe the best aspect of the course, to identify the change they would most like to see in it, and to make any other comments they wished.

Reactions to the course were generally positive: 66 per cent of respondents rated the course extremely valuable or valuable (median 2.05 on a 1 to 5 scale where 1 indicated 'extremely valuable'), 24 per cent were ambivalent and 10 per cent considered it of little or no value. Sixty-six per cent believed that the course should remain compulsory.

The division of opinion was reflected in answers to the open questions. A small minority of students made hostile comments. However, the course was strongly supported by many more students, a number of whom also identified themselves as male. A number of students said it had changed their lives or was the best course they had studied at university. The proposition that the course should *not* be taught by a man was not strongly supported in students' comments.

There was overwhelming support for the need for tutorials so that more discussion could occur. Many students noted the inhibitory effects of the large class and the tiered room. Sixty-eight per cent of respondents thought the class was too large. The same proportion, however, favoured the amount of time spent in class discussion.

As this was his first year as a university teacher, Ted was generally happy with the results of this evaluation. His concerns about the inadequacy of the forum for stimulating discussion were partly confirmed. He felt that he had maximized the possibilities for discussion, but these were significantly limited by the size of the class and by the lecture room. He resolved to continue pressing firmly for at least a limited tutorial programme the following year. He marshalled his survey data showing student support for both the compulsory nature of the course and tutorials in Legal Theory. He wrote these up in a brief report and presented them to other staff.

Ted continued his discussions with women staff members. One indicated that she might be willing to teach a Law and Gender course in conjunction with him. As an alternative, they discussed supervising honours students' seminar classes in the area, with a view to establishing a course the following year. However, in the absence of a clear commitment from any of the women staff members, Ted planned to offer the course in Feminist Legal Theory again the next year himself.

- *How well do you think Ted handled the situation?*
- *What contributing factors do you think were important in adding to his difficulties? Could he have done anything about any of these?*
- *If faced with a similar situation, how would you have acted; what would you have done differently?*

Discussion

The first point to come up in this case is the appropriateness of a man teaching a course which outlines feminist approaches to legal theory. The alternative is clearly that if Ted does not teach the course, the students will have no opportunity to encounter this subject matter. Ted openly discusses this issue with the class and it appears that there is at least one person who would prefer the subject not be taught while there are a number of others who think that it should. We know also that at the *end* of the course the general feeling is that the course was worthwhile and should be repeated. However, it may have been worthwhile for Ted to have allowed further discussion on the issue, to have brought out the arguments for and against as viewed by the students, and then to have used some mechanism for gauging the *general* class opinion on this matter. For example, there could have been a hand vote, a paper vote or response to a quickly constructed questionnaire of a couple of items which students could have completed during the class. Ted reacted very ably when the question of his credentials to teach the course was raised. He did not interpret this as a personal attack; he appeared to be cool and collected, to consider the argument against him carefully and to state his own position clearly. However, one cannot help thinking that it would have been reassuring for Ted, and would also have clarified matters for those opposed, had it been clear that the majority of the class wanted Ted to continue.

It must be said that Ted has acted pretty bravely in taking on an issue which he could foresee would be contentious, but which he considered he should not avoid. Whether or not a man *could* or in the circumstances *should* teach the course could provoke much debate among various opinions which would call themselves feminist. We can bypass this debate, however, if we accept that Ted had a clear mandate from the students and from his colleagues to teach the course. While this has not been established absolutely, it appears in all probability to be the case.

The route by which Ted found himself in this position is somewhat less clear. He is to teach a course in Legal Theory, which obviously has not considered feminist perspectives in any detail before. We are told that this is a compulsory course and so students have no choice in dropping it or continuing with it. We also know that the Faculty has 'in principle' agreed to what is presumably an optional and more specialized course concerning similar subject matter. One wonders, therefore, how these two courses became linked. In other words, why did Ted not offer to teach the Women in Law course the Faculty had approved? He was prepared to argue that being a man was insufficient reason for him not to teach such a course, so what other reasons prevented him teaching the specialist course and retaining the compulsory and generalist Legal Theory course as it was? What consideration was given to the changes which introduction of the feminist perspectives to the general course would require? What, for example, was left out of the Legal Theory course to accommodate Ted's third-term lecture series? Was the balance of this general and compulsory course considered or discussed? We can only guess at Ted's reasoning here, but if 'workload' was the sole criterion then there would seem strong grounds for Ted making a case for his workload to be adjusted, if not for this year then certainly for next.

One of the clearest signals to come from the course evaluation which Ted produced was the need for more discussion as a central part of the course. This should come as no surprise, for here we have a *third*-year course (probably of very able and articulate students) which considers content which is both interesting and contentious. The call for discussion to be a central and essential component could therefore be anticipated. Ted approaches this in two ways, first, by pressing for tutorials and second, by leaving time for discussion after he has lectured. The call for tutorials is obviously appropriate, and one could see the addition of small group discussion as being extremely valuable for this course. The students, in Ted's evaluation, further endorse this view. Ted's strategy in the large group sessions is perhaps worth considering in some more detail. Ted believes at first that the size of the group and the spatial arrangement of the lecture room preclude the possibility of discussion taking place. He later modifies this view, however, and encourages discussion after his lecture segment. One gains the impression that when Ted talks about class discussion he is talking about the whole group considering the same question at the same time, with the teacher in control of the process.

There are alternative strategies Ted could have used, however, to encourage discussion in the large group setting. For example, Ted could have displayed stimulating materials or asked a contentious question and then had the class divide up into small groups to discuss the matter. Having allowed the conversations to proceed for a reasonable time, Ted could have called for responses from discussion groups, perhaps noting the varieties of response on an overhead projector transparency. Using variants of this technique, Ted could have had anything from short and informal discussions among pairs of students, to longer and more formal presentations made by larger groups. Indeed, if Ted could have made background readings and questions available to the students before each session, most of the session could have been devoted to students talking and discussing issues. His role would thus have become redefined as 'creator of stimulating materials', motivator, facilitator and only towards the end of the session, summarizer and commentator. Those who have witnessed large group sessions in conventional lecture rooms run successfully along these lines will confirm the high level of participation, enthusiasm and interest which can be engendered in conditions which many would consider far from ideal. This is a direction in which Ted might perhaps consider moving as he plans for next year's class.

QUESTIONS FOR PERSONAL REFLECTION

- *Have you ever had your credentials to teach or to speak questioned on account of your gender? How did you feel about this? Have you ever questioned another person's credentials to teach or to speak because of his or her gender?*
- *Have you experienced the dilemma of knowing that a course is worth teaching and yet also knowing that the conditions for teaching it are far from ideal? If so, what did you do? If not, what do you think you would do in these circumstances?*
- *How do you react if you are attacked in class? Is your immediate reaction to retaliate, to retreat or to ponder the issue raised?*

- *If you have large lecture groups in a formal lecture room setting, have you experimented with approaches other than delivering a traditional lecture? Have you seen unconventional methods, such as the use of small groups, work successfully in such settings? If you have not tried or seen the use of such methods, how could you learn more about them; with whom could you discuss these things?*
- *Are there any other implications or lessons to be drawn from this case which have application in your own teaching? Is there anything in your own teaching practice that you need to reconsider after having read and reflected on this case?*

Animal Rights

Case reporter: Warren Featherston

Issues Raised

This case study raises the issue of how teachers (and departments) might respond to students who decline to take part in prescribed classes due to conscientious objection. In the incident described, objection is made to the killing of animals as part of a laboratory exercise.

Background

The Zoology Department's Animal Interactions course was a half-year course at second- or third-year level and in the year described comprised 28 students. During laboratory classes, the students worked in groups of four. When the incident occurred in the late 1980s, the teacher was in his mid-50s and had been teaching for 30 years, 20 of them at university and ten at high school.

PART ONE

Mark had been teaching parasitology at second- or third-year level for over 15 years. In the early years of teaching he had spent a considerable amount of time teaching basic parasite life-cycles. The laboratory component of the course required the examination of a variety of different species of animals which harboured parasites in order to illustrate the range of niches occupied and the various stages found in each life-cycle. Such studies were somewhat pedestrian, so to make the laboratory classes more in tune with the current emphasis in research and to make them more academically challenging, Mark introduced some physiological and biochemical experiments.

Anne was an above-average third-year student with a strong commitment to the conservation movement. She had passed her second-year examinations with high grades and was planning to undertake a fourth-year project in marine biology. The event which gave rise to the incident occurred in the third week of the course, when the group Anne was working in had to evaluate the effect of different tapeworm burdens in mice on the output of eggs from the tapeworms. Each group was supplied with mice which had been infected with either one, five or ten cysts that subsequently developed into tapeworms over a two-week period. They were also supplied with the faeces produced by each mouse over the previous 24-hour period. The laboratory exercise required an assessment of egg output in the faeces using standard methods followed by an examination of the mouse's gut to determine the actual number of tapeworms present.

Mark had, prior to the laboratory session, anaesthetized the mice and broken their necks so that the students were presented with properly killed specimens. Anne took one look at the specimens and said, 'I do not agree with the killing of animals for experimental purposes. I will not take any further part in this exercise'.

- *What do you think happened next?*
- *What would you have done if you had been in Mark's position?*

PART TWO

After a brief tirade on animal rights to the group, Anne prepared to walk out of the class. Mark agreed that Anne could leave the class, but he asked her to come and see him later in the week to discuss the matter. The rest of the class went off without any problems, but the remaining students showed an interest in what Mark's course of action would be.

At the meeting with Anne, Mark pointed out that besides missing out on a significant class, she was missing an assessment grade. While he could appreciate her stand on grounds of conscience, he felt that she should do an extra numerical assignment based on some previous work of a similar nature. Anne agreed to undertake this work.

Because of this incident, Mark raised the matter at a staff meeting and after much discussion it was agreed that time should be made available at the first laboratory session each year to point out to students the ethical guidelines under which animals were used for experimental purposes. Any students with genuine conscientious objections were to be informed that they should make these known to the head of department. If such students wished to be excused from exercises involving live animal experimentation, they would be required to undertake extra work assignments set by the lecturers.

- *How satisfactory do you think the outcome was for the student, the teacher and the department?*
- *Were there any other options open to the people involved? If so, what were some of them and what might have been the consequences of taking them?*
- *Would you have done anything differently?*

Discussion

The main issue in this case is obviously the response of a teacher (and department) to the moral stance taken by a student when she refuses to participate in a set exercise because she objects on the grounds of conscience. While the sequel and the long-term response seem to have been worked through amicably enough, it is worthwhile considering some further possible interpretations of the situation and reactions to it.

The teacher and the department in the case study appear to have taken the incident at face value and reacted in a moderate fashion. Others might have responded differently. For instance, some might have wondered if Anne was simply a troublemaker intent on stirring up a confrontation, or a lazy student looking for excuses to avoid work. The facts that Anne was 'above average', had 'passed her second-year examinations with high grades', was 'planning to undertake a fourth-year project', and was known to have a 'strong commitment to the conservation movement', could all be interpreted as strengthening her own credibility and assisting her case. Would the case be so compelling if Anne had been perceived as a weak student or if her attitude was considered little more than a whim? The circumstances and context within which moral issues are debated are always important and the credibility of the actual person making the case is often crucial, irrespective of the strength of the case itself. In this case, Anne's credibility and the sincerity of her objection were taken for granted. This may not always be so.

The actual nature of Anne's objections were never made specific. Presumably a different lecturer may have held equally strong and defensible views on the *necessity* of animal experimentation for scientific and medical progress. Would Anne consider animal experimentation to be unacceptable under *any* circumstances, or was her position that this experiment for purely teaching purposes was unnecessary? Perhaps Anne feels that behavioural studies (as possibly for her fourth-year project) offer the only acceptable approach. But does this avoid the moral question of animal rights with respect to humans altering and affecting 'natural' behaviour by the simple act of observation? How far has Anne (and her lecturer) thought these things through and would further dialogue between them be beneficial in terms of reaching a greater degree of clarification and mutual understanding?

Power in a confrontation such as this is often stacked heavily on the side of the lecturer and the department. The teacher or the department could have taken a stricter stance on what would happen. They could have insisted that the student do the experiment and, if she refused, she could have been penalized for missing the class. This could have been justified in a number of ways. The fact that the class was included in the curriculum indicates that the lecturer considered it important. Perhaps he considered it more than this, a *vital* aspect of the course. Should the lecturer, according to *his* conscience, allow a student to decide which parts of the curriculum are important, which parts to complete and which parts not to complete? Is every or any moral or conscientious position to be allowed as valid? Or does higher education (or in this case, scientific experimentation) demand that its practitioners hold a common set of value positions? How far then do students or dissidents have the right to question such value positions and to effect change? There are some basic questions here on the rights and responsibilities of both lecturers and students, and the means by which communication between them on matters such as this is promoted and advanced.

A further question relates to fairness with regard to the others in the class. If Anne has successfully negotiated an alternative to the standard curriculum, should this possibility also be offered to the other class members? Is it the lecturer's duty to bring up this possibility, or was he right to assume a more reactive stance? Negotiation of the curriculum and the pursuit of student autonomy and self-direction are often considered to be progressive educational ideas; could or should the lecturer have taken the opportunity presented by this issue to move in such directions? Could the class as a whole have benefited from an opening-up of the issue for discussion or even class-based decision-making? Could Anne have been asked to outline her case and suggest alternative activities that would help students to achieve similar objectives and learn the same material as effectively without requiring the activities to which she objects? While it is likely that a course of action similar to the one taken would have been arrived at in each of these instances, these other methods could give students more of a say in the matter and remove the appearance of power, control and unilateral decision-making from the 'authorities'.

In short, an acceptable, realistic solution appears to have been arrived at that would probably cause little resentment among conscientious objectors or the others in the class. However, the bases upon which the decision have been made appear to be far from clear and the department might well reflect upon questions such as the following: can all questions of conscience be accommodated; how are those which can and those which cannot to be distinguished; how far is individual exception to be tolerated or encouraged in a course and whose responsibility is it to raise this matter; how are moral and ethical differences between teachers and students to be resolved within the classroom? Departments in which incidents like the one in the case study could arise would be well advised to have considered the issues in advance and to have at least the framework of a policy and some guidance for lecturers in place.

QUESTIONS FOR PERSONAL REFLECTION

- *Are you and is your department prepared for incidents analogous to the one described in this case study?*
- *How do you and how does your department feel about students who lodge conscientious objections to components of courses? Are students made aware of departmental policy?*
- *Have you and has your department considered the ramifications of the agreed or* de facto *policy which is in place? Should you act 'reactively' only or should you play a leadership role in bringing such issues and possibilities to the attention of classes?*
- *After having read and reflected upon this case, do you see any other implications for any course or courses that you or your department teach?*

The Shared Course

Case reporter: The person who reported this case wishes to remain anonymous

---

Issues Raised

The issues raised by this case concern the dilemma faced by a teacher when made aware of student dissatisfaction with the teaching of a colleague. How can the teacher act so as not to alienate either the students or the colleague? Other issues concern the evaluation of teaching or of courses by students and by others.

Background

The incident which is described occurred in the late 1980s. At the time, the teachers were both around 40 years old. Arthur had about nine years of teaching experience; Charlie about four years. It was the first time that either of them had taught the course involved. The case reporter comments: 'The relationship between Arthur and Charlie precluded discussion of the problem'.

PART ONE

Background to the incident

Arthur Baker and Charlie Deacon were both lecturers in a small department in a university Faculty of Science. Academic performance had traditionally been measured using the tried and trusted 'publish or perish' rule, but it was rumoured that teaching performance would in future be taken into account as well, particularly for confirmation of tenure and for promotion. Arthur regarded the importance given to numbers of publications as exaggerated and welcomed the rumoured development.

The question of the methods to be applied in evaluating teaching performance was, however, a source of worry. Arthur had little confidence in evaluation by peers: none of the staff in the department had any significant formal training in teaching or lecturing. In this respect a colleague with, say, 20 years' teaching experience could often be regarded as having had one year's experience repeated 20 times over. In addition, he felt that their knowledge of what went on in other people's lectures was often sketchy. Evaluation by persons skilled in evaluating teaching was a possibility, but a query was whether their lack of knowledge about the subject being taught would make much of a difference. Evaluation by students was regarded as a feasible option, and Arthur had in fact made a practice in the past of canvassing students' opinions on his courses and on his teaching. He found this useful both for the purpose of improving his courses and to submit with applications for promotion.

The course

Arthur and Charlie were sharing a third-year course, attended by just under 40 students. The course content was technical, involving a considerable amount of mathematics in a number of areas. It was the first time that Arthur had shared a course with anyone else. The work was shared more or less equally, but Charlie was the course coordinator. Shortly after the start of lectures in the year in question, the head of the department announced that a number of guest lecturers would be available to assist with courses in the department, and one was assigned to take a substantial block of lectures in the course concerned, with a second taking some other lectures.

During the first term, Arthur and Charlie shared lectures by assigning two to Arthur and one to Charlie each week. Once the arrangements for the guest lecturers had firmed up, Arthur requested all three weekly lectures, so that a suitable break point in his part of the course could be reached. Charlie agreed to this, so Arthur was able to stop his lectures at a reasonably logical point at the end of term one. He did not see the class again until the third term; lectures during the intervening period were taken by Charlie and the guest lecturers.

The problems

When Arthur took up lectures again during the third term in order to complete his part of the course, he sensed that the class was dissatisfied. He was not, however, prepared for the hostility which became apparent three weeks later when he made an announcement to the class on Charlie's behalf at the start of one of the lectures. It was apparent that the hostility was directed mainly at Charlie, but it was also due in part to the disruption caused by the fact that the guest lecturers had become available at a relatively late stage. Arthur made a plea to the class 'not to kill the messenger' and the atmosphere relaxed. Private discussions with some members of the class revealed that Arthur's impression had not been wrong; the dissatisfaction was deep and apparently widespread. Arthur faced two problems. First, how could the students, who obviously felt that they had been short-changed, be helped? Second, Arthur was planning to ask the students to complete a standard teaching evaluation questionnaire, but he was worried about the effect that the students' dissatisfaction would have on their evaluation of his own teaching. What should he do about the two problems?

- *What do you think Arthur did next with respect to his two problems?*
- *What would you have done at this point?*

PART TWO

The meeting

Arthur discussed the problem with Edward Fogarty, a senior colleague whose opinions he respected. Edward was already aware of the problem and told Arthur that the students were also concerned that the content of another course was out of date. He had advised the class representative to set up a meeting with the head of department (HOD). This was done, and as a result a meeting open to all of the students and attended by the HOD and Edward was organized. Arthur did not attend the meeting, but he was told by Edward that there had been a full and frank discussion. It is not known what, if anything, the HOD said to Charlie or to the lecturer in charge of the 'outdated' course, but the students did settle down for the remainder of the year. Arthur did not see any immediate need to take the matter further for the students' sake.

The questionnaires

The problem of obtaining an unbiased evaluation of his own performance was tackled by Arthur giving the students two questionnaires to fill out at the same time. One was headed with the title of the course, followed by his own name, while the other was simply headed with the title of the course. Arthur asked the students to fill in the two questionnaires, to make an attempt to evaluate *his* teaching performance in one questionnaire, and to use the other questionnaire to evaluate *the remainder of the course*. The students agreed to do this, and the questionnaires were processed in two separate lots in the usual way. Arthur was reasonably satisfied with the evaluation of his performance as indicated by the results of the first questionnaire. He found that many students had written comments on the back of the second questionnaire form. They were generally critical of the overall organization of the course and of Charlie's lectures and laboratory classes, but satisfied with the lectures given by the two guest lecturers.

- *How well do you think Arthur handled this incident?*
- *If faced with a similar incident, how would you have acted; what would you have done differently?*

Discussion

The central concern of this case is the dilemma faced by Arthur when students express their dissatisfaction with the teaching of his colleague, Charlie, with whom he is sharing a course. What should Arthur do? If he does nothing, then he can hope that the problem might simply disappear.

However, it may grow worse, and by failing to act Arthur may alienate the students and dissatisfaction with the course may grow. Should this happen, it would mean that Arthur too will face the consequences, and this is of some concern to him as he wants to obtain a good teaching evaluation in order to assist him to advance. On the other hand, Arthur could take some action, perhaps suggesting to the students that they approach Charlie with the problem. Alternatively, he could consider broaching the subject with Charlie or with someone else in the department. We know from the background material that the relationship between Arthur and Charlie is such that Arthur feels he cannot approach Charlie. This then is Arthur's dilemma, and it seems there is no *safe* way for him to act in order to extricate himself.

If faced with this situation, many teachers would take the easy option and do nothing, reasoning that the problem may sort itself out anyway and that the risk of alienating one's colleague, with whom one has to live year in and year out, is harder to justify than the risk of alienating a particular group of students. It would seem a pity, however, if inertia won out as the only safe course of action, since accepting the present conditions to be in some way 'natural' or unalterable precludes the possibility of development and improvement. However, recommending a more positive course of action in the present case is rendered difficult, as throughout the case we are given no idea of what it is that the students are complaining about on Charlie's part of the course. It may be that they have some rather minor complaint which has become blown out of proportion and which could easily be put right. On the other hand, it may be that the problem is deep-seated, requiring long-term and possibly outside intervention. It may be a problem with which Charlie is quite familiar and which he has chosen to ignore for the time being or it may be a problem of which he is quite unaware and which he would find devastating, should it emerge. Without knowing something about the nature of the problem which the students perceive, one's ability to comment is thus limited.

That having been said, in most circumstances the positive course of action which is perhaps least intrusive and safest as a first step would be to suggest to the students that they raise their concerns with Charlie himself. Building communication between teacher and students is obviously fundamental to the process of teaching, and the root of many problems in teaching can be traced to a failure of communication. If the students can raise their concerns with Charlie, seeking not to chastise and blame but rather to find solutions to their problems, then the outcomes for themselves and for Charlie could be equally positive. This could perhaps be Arthur's best immediate response.

Should that course of action not resolve the problem, Arthur's next remedy is probably the very one he rules out as being impossible, namely, to raise the matter with Charlie. If Arthur and Charlie could find some shared experience and work toward mutual understandings, there is the potential for everyone involved in the case to gain. It seems that Arthur and Charlie are able at least to speak to each other, as they have managed to organize the course, seemingly, amicably enough. Could this be built on by Arthur suggesting that they discuss how the course is going and how they could go about finding this out? Arthur might care to share with Charlie the concerns and problems *he* has experienced with his part of the course before inviting Charlie to do the same. If Arthur can persuade Charlie that they both share responsibility for the course, and that any action they take will be joint and non-threatening to Charlie, perhaps they will be able to move forward. One good strategy in this regard is for them to run a *course* evaluation questionnaire, rather than *teacher* evaluation questionnaires. This they could formulate, carry out, discuss and evaluate together. They would be cooperating for the good of the course, rather than competing in the 'best teacher' stakes. Arthur, however, could still carry out his own teaching evaluation, which would remain private and solely for use in his personal application for advancement.

Arthur's actual course of action was not along either of these lines. His first step was to discuss the problem with a senior colleague, who then involved the student class representative and the head of department. Unfortunately, we know nothing of what took place between the students, Charlie, and the head of department, except for the fact that things cooled down afterwards. Again, we have no idea of how far the 'outdated' course (which had nothing to do with Arthur or Charlie) was responsible for the students' dissatisfaction or whether this was a red herring. Although Arthur was not directly responsible for calling in the head of department and this may have happened anyway, Arthur preferred to involve others rather than the students and the person directly involved. As it was, the students and Charlie had the opportunity to sort out their differences under the aegis of the head of department. It is perhaps a shame that they could not have done so without involving Arthur, Edward and the HOD. Arthur says that it was impossible for him to talk to Charlie, but one is left with the impression that no matter how difficult this might have been, often the most difficult actions are those which are most needed. If handled sensitively, even a slight improvement in the relationship between Arthur and Charlie would have augured well for this course in future years.

The other interesting aspect of the case is the process Arthur goes through in deciding how to evaluate his teaching. Independently, he arrives at the conclusion that student evaluation of teaching is a sound method. The curious thing about this to those who work in educational development is that many teachers in Arthur's position have the same concerns, and they too do not think of seeking advice. Had Arthur approached an educational or staff development professional with his enquiry, he could have been directed to good summaries of the large theoretical and empirical literature on this subject. From this he could have confirmed the validity and reliability of student evaluation of teaching. The unfortunate thing is that many teachers start from a different view (particularly concerning student evaluation of teaching) but never confront the research evidence available. Again, had Arthur been introduced to the research literature he would have been relieved to find that, as long as the questionnaire is properly constructed, his fears of students not being able to distinguish their opinions concerning *his* teaching from their concerns over other aspects of the course were also unfounded. Having worried about this when he came to take the survey, he found that the actual results confirmed countless other surveys which have shown similar results: students are quite capable of independently and analytically judging a particular teacher's practice together with different aspects of that practice.

A final word has to be said on the ethical position of Arthur in connection with the student evaluations of teaching which he ran. The circumstances under which student evaluations are taken vary quite markedly between institutions. Some institutions now make it compulsory for staff to undertake student evaluations and have a system which takes the responsibility for initiating these out of the hands of staff members. Results too may go not only to the member of staff concerned, but also to the head of department and others in the management hierarchy. It is conceivable given these circumstances that members of staff do not even know whether or when they are being evaluated. This seems very unfortunate, as it takes the responsibility for monitoring and evaluation of their professional practice out of the hands of individuals, thus alienating them from the process, making it at the same time more of a process of control and less one of normal professional responsibility.

Arthur's action in having students evaluate Charlie (by default), and without his prior knowledge or consent, would seem to be equally ill-advised and unethical. There was little that Arthur could use the information for anyway, other than to see whether the evaluation of teaching he received was higher than that given for the other parts of the course. He could not use this to support his own case, however, and none of the information which could have proved valuable for diagnosing what was wrong with the course as a whole or with Charlie's part of it could be used. The original suggestion, therefore, of Arthur and Charlie working together on constructing and analysing a *course* evaluation questionnaire may have proven far more beneficial.

QUESTIONS FOR PERSONAL REFLECTION

- *Have you ever experienced a situation similar to the one described by Arthur, in which students criticize a course or part of a course being taken by one of your colleagues? What did you do?*
- *Have you ever experienced the situation where a colleague has informed you of student criticism of your course or teaching? What did you do? Could you have handled the situation more constructively?*
- *Do you have colleagues with whom you have to interact, but with whom you find it very difficult to communicate? Is there anything you can do to improve such relationships, any course matters on which you can work together cooperatively?*
- *What are your beliefs concerning student evaluation of teaching? Do you*

consider such evaluations to be valid and reliable? Do you consider other ways of evaluating teaching to be preferable? Have you read any of the summaries of research carried out in this area? If not, should you?

- *Are there any other implications or lessons to be drawn from this case which have application in your own teaching? Is there anything in your own teaching practice that you need to reconsider after having read and reflected on this case?*

The Case of the Emotional Professor

Case reporter: Colin Watts

Issues Raised

The issue which is apparently raised by this case is what happens to both a teacher and students in a class where an incident in class provokes a drastic response from the teacher. Behind the incident, however, the central issue concerns the building of rapport between the teacher and students. There are other aspects to the case including the intervention of cultural differences, language difficulties, and the notions that teachers are emotionally detached from what happens in their classes and that they adhere to a stereotyped image of how a teacher behaves.

Background

The person who prepared this case study was a student in the class in which the incident occurred. The teacher was in his 40s at the time, had been teaching for a number of years and was a highly regarded research worker in his field. The students were mostly 20 or 21 years old. The episode occurred in the late 1950s at one of the newer universities in England.

PART ONE

The course and the class

The incident occurred during a physiology presentation in the third and final year of an ordinary Bachelor of Science degree, with physiology being one of the major subjects. The class usually consisted of about 40 science students, but at this particular presentation there was an approximately equal number of medical students present. The two groups of students had not previously had such a combined teaching session.

Neurophysiology was the subject being taught. The science students were having problems with this subject, which was proving especially difficult for a number of reasons such as the inherent complexity of the subject, the lack of knowledge of anatomy (which was not taught to these students), and problems with the particular lecturer's ability to communicate.

The lecturer

Professor Portriga was a senior staff member of the Department of Physiology. He was Italian and his standard of spoken English was not very good, to say the least. This caused quite severe problems for his lectures. He was obviously aware of the difficulty and this made him very nervous; of course, this nervousness did not help the situation. He also had a 'Latin temperament', which came through as a high degree of emotional involvement with his teaching. It would be fair to say that the students did not like his lectures and it appeared that Professor Portriga did not like giving them.

The incident

For this combined presentation, Professor Portriga was to show an educational film to illustrate material given in a previous lecture. It concerned patients who had severe neuro-motor disease or brain lesions which affected their movements and coordination. After a short introduction by the nervous professor, the film started. Eventually, patients with grossly exaggerated and often bizarre, uncontrolled movements were seen. At this stage, several students in one section of the class started to laugh at some of the strange actions being shown. This laughter increased as the film progressed and the laughing spread to other areas of the class.

At that point, Professor Portriga abruptly stopped the film and put on the lights. He was obviously angry and greatly distressed. Although he could barely speak coherently, he managed to convey to the class that he was not prepared to teach a 'pack of animals' and that he was abandoning the course in neurophysiology at that point. He then departed and left the class in stunned silence.

- *What would you have done if you were the teacher faced with this situation?*
- *What do you think happened next?*

PART TWO

A small group of about six science students immediately went to find Professor Portriga to apologize for the behaviour of the class. He was sitting in his office, obviously still upset, and he appeared to have been crying. He accepted the apology and, in fact, spent quite a long time talking about the course and his problems.

He continued with his lectures and, although there were still communication problems, there was an improvement in his rapport with the class, probably because the students became more aware of him as a person and of his difficulties.

- *Can you explain why this incident occurred?*
- *How would you have acted had you been in Professor Portriga's place? What would you have done differently?*

Discussion

Although this is a fairly short case, it raises a number of issues. Of central importance is the nature of the relationship between Professor Portriga and his students. It seems that the relationship is not a happy one from either point of view. The students find that his standard of English and probably his foreign accent make the lectures difficult to follow. Professor Portriga is probably aware of such deficiencies and this would fuel his nervousness. This nervousness in turn may well contribute to his lack of fluency and thus we have a seemingly closed circle of discomfort for both teacher and students. There seems to be no level of personal contact, let alone rapport or empathy, between teacher and students until the incident has occurred. Perhaps the most pertinent questions we can ask, therefore, are why this is so and why the incident which occurred caused things to change.

Many teachers, perhaps including Professor Portriga, have a stereotyped image of how a teacher should behave, how a teacher should act and be. Professor Portriga's stereotype may well have been shaped by the time of the incident, occurring as it did in the 1950s, and also by the fact that as a foreigner he may have tried to model what he considered appropriate behaviour from the English colleagues he observed at this time. We could imagine his stereotype being such that the teacher is seen as aloof, resolute, in control of the subject matter and absolutely in control of demeanour and emotion. Teaching in the lecture room should thus be a serious, 'strait-laced' and unemotional affair, and students should bear their share of the responsibility for ensuring this is so.

Why is it that many teachers seek to hide their own personality, their vitality, individuality, humour and emotion behind a facade such as this? Perhaps it is no more than the impression that this is how one *should* behave, but perhaps too it lies in an insecurity that in some way one is not really good enough, that one cannot therefore afford to reveal oneself as an individual, and so it is safer to hide one's true self behind a stereotypical screen. If Professor Portriga feels himself to have such inadequacies (concerning his spoken English, accent and general 'cultural discomfort' with his students), then we begin to see why he could have cut himself off from any human interaction with his class and why he has failed to build any rapport.

We might ask the question at this point whether he could have done anything to build rapport with his class right from the beginning. The answer to this is obviously 'Yes', and had he done so, the incident which occurred may not have caused such a strong reaction. Had Professor Portriga shown some of himself as a human being to his students, then they may have appreciated *his* problems more fully and made greater allowance. For example, Professor Portriga could have made his problems with English into a game of the sort: 'I will teach you what I know of neurophysiology; will you please help me with my English explanations?' Getting the students involved in such a dialogue could have two benefits. First, the resentment caused by students failing to understand what was being said and explained could be averted as students would have felt more comfortable in intervening when necessary during the lecture until they had a clear understanding. Second, with teacher and students actually talking to each other and seeking shared explanations, each would be more likely to break the stereotypical view they would have formed at the beginning. The students would have seen that there was more to Professor Portriga than simply 'unintelligible foreigner' and Professor Portriga would have been less inclined to stereotype his students as a 'pack of animals'.

The interesting point is that when Professor Portriga *did* break out of stereotype by showing his humanity, his anger, frustration and emotion, the students responded positively and an improvement in rapport was reported. This began when the small delegation of students found him and apologized for the incident, and Portriga opened up, probably talking 'person-to-person' with these students and regarding them as individuals for the very first time. Again, it is a pity that such building of rapport could not have started earlier and that this unfortunate incident was necessary to act as a catalyst.

As to the incident itself, it is perhaps worth putting oneself in the place of the students. Some readers may be horrified that the students found something to laugh at in the film they were watching, while others would have to admit that in similar circumstances they too could well have been drawn into the laughter. There is perhaps something in this to do with the nature of 'English' humour, a humour which often takes pleasure in its 'difference' and its ability to laugh at situations which others would consider sacrosanct. There may also be something in the circumstances before the film was shown. From the account of the circumstances we know that the teacher was very nervous and so, too, in all probability, were many of the students. In an atmosphere of nervous tension, laughter is one of the most potent of forces. Experienced teachers often use humour as a device to release tension in such situations. In this incident, the release came from the students, but the result was quite unanticipated.

Could Portriga have handled the situation better when it arose? Almost certainly he could, in that breaking off dialogue and making threats is seldom helpful in such circumstances. Had he developed some rapport with the students previously he may have been able to talk about what happened, and perhaps to have appreciated that the clip could legitimately be seen as both tragic and comic at the same time. The students' initial reaction could even have been built into his dialogue with them about how people react to seeing such conditions and what the consequences are. We can only hope that Professor Portriga has learned something from the incident and that he would be less likely to dissociate himself from his students in future. From the students' point of view, too, it seems likely that they have learned to appreciate something of the individuality and humanity of one of their teachers.

QUESTIONS FOR PERSONAL REFLECTION

- *Do you actively try to build rapport with each new class you take? If so, how do you do this; what exactly do you do? If not, how could you do this, what could you do? If you do not believe in building rapport, what kinds of messages are your students receiving about you at the beginning of your courses?*
- *Have you ever encountered a situation in your own teaching where you were disgusted with student behaviour during a class? How did you react? Would you have done things differently having now had more time to consider the incident more carefully?*
- *Do you have any colleagues who you think may be facing the kinds of difficulties encountered in this case? Would they welcome your friendship? Is there anything you might be able to do to assist them?*
- *Are there any other implications or lessons to be drawn from this case which have application in your own teaching? Is there anything in your own teaching practice that you need to reconsider after having read and reflected on this case?*

Annotated Bibliography

Introduction

The origins of this annotated bibliography lie in the seminars for staff development which are described in the appendix. Readings were recommended to those who participated in these seminars in addition to the case studies included in this book. Some of the original readings remain, but they have been supplemented by a number of others which we hope may prove useful to teachers unfamiliar with some of the resources which are available with regard to helping to improve teaching and learning. The items have been grouped into four categories: More Cases; Teaching Handbooks and Resources; Group Discussion Methods; Reflective Practice. We should emphasize, however, that there is no intention to be comprehensive in the materials we have listed, and some of them could be considered positively quirky. We hope you enjoy them.

More cases

If you enjoyed the idea of considering case studies of situations which have actually confronted teachers in higher education, here are two further items you might want to look up.

- **New Perspectives on Teaching and Learning**
Warren Bryan Martin (ed.), New Directions for Teaching and Learning Series, No. 7, San Francisco, CA: Jossey-Bass, 1981.

   This paperback volume, one in a useful series on teaching and learning, contains 37 personal statements written by American teachers who responded to an invitation to prepare case studies for discussion at a conference on teaching and learning. Virtually all of the writers had been successful in national competitions for prestigious teaching fellowships and thus were 'aware of the importance of teaching, have been reflective and self-critical about their own professional lives, and have contributions to make in this ongoing discussion about teaching and learning ....' (p. 3). The case studies are divided into three thematic sections, each of which is accompanied by a commentary and criticism by a renowned teacher. The case studies encompass a wide array of teaching situations and they are candid and thought-provoking. On the other hand, many are extremely brief, each is written as a single part only, and there is little specific commentary beyond the writer's own reflections. Within these constraints, however, these case studies have much to offer, in large part because of the calibre of the writers and their commitment to teaching.

- **Teaching and the Case Method. Text, Cases, and Readings *and* Teaching and the Case Method. Instructor's Guide**
C Roland Christensen, Boston, MA: Harvard Business School, 1987.

These two fairly large volumes were prepared as part of Harvard Business School's programme of seminars to introduce newcomers to the School's case method style of teaching. In order to do this, case studies of *teaching* are used in the seminars, with the materials for the case studies being provided by people who have attended the seminars. The case studies deal with a variety of problems in teaching. Many are long and elaborate, most are in multiple parts, and there are extensive commentaries accompanying them. However, the cases were designed for use in seminars to demonstrate the case method of teaching and so the commentaries are directed as much to the mechanics of discussing the cases as to the issues raised. Because of this, individual readers may not get as much out of the case studies as they might if the commentaries had been designed to help individuals reflect on the issues raised and what conclusions they can draw for their own practice. Having said that, the case studies *do* provide much food for thought for those who acquire the two books, both of which are required to obtain the complete versions of most of the case studies.

Teaching handbooks and resources

Here are some books and resources which may prove of immediate use to those looking for practical ideas and stimulation for their own teaching.

● **Interesting Ways to Teach**
Various combinations of Graham Gibbs, Trevor Habeshaw and Sue Habeshaw, including: *Preparing to Teach; 53 Interesting Things to Do in Your Lectures; 53 Interesting Things to Do in Your Seminars and Tutorials; 53 Interesting Ways to Assess Your Students; 53 Interesting Ways of Helping Your Students to Study; 53 Interesting Ways to Appraise Your Teaching; 253 Ideas for Your Teaching*. All titles are Bristol: Technical and Educational Services Ltd, 1984–92.

These titles are part of an expanding series of books which contain a wealth of practical suggestions that teachers might like to try as part of their efforts to improve their own teaching and their students' learning. To quote the authors in *Preparing to Teach*: 'We are interested in teaching methods which address real problems in practical ways, and which leave lecturers feeling comfortable about how they are behaving, (p. 15). The suggestions are presented concisely, they are eminently practicable, and they tend to conform with the authors' preferences for emphasizing the roles of the learner and learning rather than the teacher and teaching (see *Better teaching or better learning?* later in this bibliography). You will almost certainly find that there is a large degree of variation in the extent to which the '53' items of each book are useful, but if five or six items prove valuable in changing the nature of your teaching practice, then the book will have been worthwhile.

● **Effective Learning and Teaching in Higher Education**
Various authors, Committee of Vice Chancellors and Principals, Universities' Staff Development Unit, University of Sheffield, 1992.

This is a series of twelve modules, each of three parts. Part 1 takes you through some basic material on each topic; questions are posed and space is provided for your responses. Part 2 contains examples in which the basic material is translated into different subject areas. Part 3 provides suggestions and resources for running workshops on the topic. As with any series, there is some variability in the standard of the modules, but overall there is a lot of useful and accessible material in the series which should be valuable to both teachers and staff developers alike. The topics are: What is active learning?; Course design for active learning; Planning teaching for active learning; Active learning in large classes and with increasing student numbers; Enabling active learning in small groups; Active learning in practical classes; Active learning in field work and project work; Learning actively on one's own; Essay writing for active learning; Promoting the development of personal and professional skills; Assessing active learning; Evaluating teaching and courses from an active learning perspective.

● **HERDSA Green Guides**
Various authors, Higher Education Research and Development Society of Australasia, Tertiary Education Research Centre, University of New South Wales, Australia, 1984–92.

HERDSA Green Guides are well known throughout Australasia and the UK. The older ones have been around for a time now, but some have been revised and new titles are continually being added. Although they are not 'interactive' in the same way as the 'Effective Learning and Teaching in Higher Education' series, they do contain much valuable material on a variety of topics. These include: Reviewing departments; Up the publication road; Supervising postgraduates; Improving student writing; Implementing student self-assessment; Conducting tutorials; Lecturing; Assessing student performance; and Heading a department.

● **A Handbook for Teachers in Universities and Colleges (Revised edition)**
David Newble and Robert Cannon, London: Kogan Page, 1991.

Based on an earlier book for medical teachers, this addition to the 'Handbook' literature contains useful practical advice on both traditional and more innovative teaching methods. It has sections on teaching in large groups; making a presentation at a conference; teaching in small groups; teaching practical and laboratory classes; curriculum planning; assessing students; preparing teaching materials and using teaching aids; helping students learn. It has many illustrations and practical tips and is written in a lively style which is easy to follow. It deals very briefly with some of the 'educational principles' which are thought to underlie the practices advocated, and there is a short and useful annotated bibliography at the end of each chapter.

● **College Teaching**
A journal published quarterly by HELDREF Publications, a division of the Helen Dwight Reid Educational Foundation, 1319 Eighteenth Street, NW, Washington, DC 20036–1802.

The articles in this journal are easy to follow and include both practical and more philosophical items. There are also commentaries, brief practical suggestions ('The Quick Fix'), and reviews of many books that may be of interest to teachers in higher education. There is almost always something of immediate interest and/or of practical use in each issue.

● **The Teaching Professor**
A newsletter published ten times a year by Magna Publications Inc., 2718 Dryden Drive, Madison, WI 53704–3086.

This is a six to eight page newsletter which tries to keep busy teachers in higher education aware of important issues in teaching and to provide useful ideas for teaching practice. It consists of a series of short items which may be philosophical or practical. Some of these are contributed by readers, some are prepared by the editor, and others are digests from the literature in the general areas of teaching and education. Many of the ideas stimulate thought or further study, and the format ensures that the contents can be quickly absorbed.

- **The Craft of Teaching (2nd edition)**
Kenneth E Eble, San Francisco, CA: Jossey-Bass, 1988.
   Proclaimed as one of the best books ever published on the topic of college teaching, this book does not just give a list of tips on 'how to do it' but instead takes a more philosophical stance. The author thus talks to his readers and offers friendly advice while at the same time mentioning things that we should think about as we develop as teachers. In keeping with this approach, his sections on 'The Mythology of Teaching'; 'Cheating, Confrontations, and Other Situations'; and 'Motivating Students and Faculty' are down-to-earth, enlightening and unlike most of what is typically found in many other guidebooks to teaching.

- **Learning to Teach in Higher Education**
Paul Ramsden, London: Routledge, 1992.
   While the aim of this book is to help improve the standard of teaching in higher education, it takes an unusual approach towards that aim. Unlike guidebooks which concentrate on the techniques of instruction, Ramsden attempts to get teachers to take into account in their teaching a consideration of learning by their students. From this he derives principles for effective teaching and goes on from these to show how the application of these principles can improve learning, using case studies for illustration. Although he is uncompromising in his approach and makes a number of assertions with which we disagree, he provides many good arguments and valuable ideas. The book should be especially stimulating to teachers who are willing to be convinced of what is still an atypical notion of the role of the teacher in higher education.

Group discussion methods

In the previous section were a number of series or sources which contained valuable information on teaching and learning using group discussion methods (such as tutorials, seminars, project groups, case-based and problem-based learning, for example). Here are two more items which go into considerably more detail on this topic.

- **Learning in Groups (Second edition)**
David Jaques, London: Kogan Page, 1991.
   This book provides many useful insights into what is going on in your groups as well as giving some good practical suggestions for running them better. The early chapters on the psychology of group behaviour (or individuals' behaviours in groups) are particularly interesting. The theories outlined there are contentious, but if you are unfamiliar with this area, the insights afforded here may prove useful in trying to work out what is at the root of particular problems being exhibited by a group. As with the cases in *our* book, more of this than you might have thought can often be traced back to the tutor. The more 'applied' sections give good, practical advice; there is a section of case studies which give examples of group learning in many subject areas, and finally a section on 'training' methods and activities which both teachers and staff developers might find useful.

- **Small Group Teaching: A Trouble-Shooting Guide**
Richard G Tiberius, Toronto: Ontario Institute for Studies in Education, 1990.
   This is a self-proclaimed 'do-it-yourself' trouble-shooting manual for teaching in small groups. It identifies a series of the most important problems that can arise in small group work, possible causes of the problems, and suggestions for what might

be done to deal with them. The book's main sections are on group goals, group interaction and group motivation and emotion. The author includes many actual examples from his own experience as a teaching consultant to illustrate his points about the sorts of problems that could arise and methods for resolving them.

Reflective practice

The materials in this section lead on from the latter items of the 'Teaching Handbooks and Resources' section above. There, the notion of developing as a teacher and improving teaching and learning was treated as a process, rather than a series of 'tips' or 'tricks' to be learned and applied. We are of the opinion that to alienate teaching practices from teaching theories, and the values which underlie them, is to diminish both. We believe that practice and theory are inextricably bound together along with our most basic values concerning the enterprise of teaching and our own humanity. In this section are some stimulating materials on this theme.

- **Better teaching or better learning?**

Graham Gibbs, *HERDSA News*, 1983, 5(2), 3–6, 11.

   This is one of our favourite articles and it has regularly been among the readings which we distribute at our seminars and workshops on teaching. It is a hard hitting, heavily biased attack on the lecture as it is experienced in higher education. It both encourages and challenges teachers to think about giving more weight to students and learning than to teachers and teaching. It is a stimulating and provocative challenge to the widely held view of what properly constitutes the teacher's role in higher education.

- **Personal theories of teaching**

Dennis Fox, *Studies in Higher Education*, 1983, 8(2), 151–63.

   This classic paper, a must for all teachers, outlines some of the personal theories (or metaphors) which people use when they think about teaching. Read it and see which theory (transfer, shaping, travelling or growing) you tend to use yourself. For another highly readable description of teaching metaphors see: 'Coaching and playing right field. Trying on metaphors for teaching', Robert J Kloss, *College Teaching*, 1987, 35(4), 134–9.

- **Teaching as a Subversive Activity**

Neil Postman and Charles Weingartner, Harmondsworth: Penguin Books, 1969.

   This is another gem which, despite being written for the American school system, has much relevance for higher education throughout the world. If you are pushed for time (or want to recommend a single reading from the book), start with Chapter 2: 'The medium is the message, of course'. There you will find the following attempt to summarize the *real* messages students may receive from us (pp. 31–2):

   Passive acceptance is a more desirable response to ideas than active criticism. Discovering knowledge is beyond the power of students .... Recall is the highest form of intellectual achievement .... The voice of authority is to be trusted and valued more than independent judgment. One's own ideas and those of one's classmates are inconsequential. Feelings are irrelevant in education. There is always a single, unambiguous Right Answer to a question.... a subject is something you 'take' and, when you have taken it, you have 'had' it, and if you have 'had' it, you are immune and need not take it again. (The Vaccination Theory of Education?)

- **Freedom to Learn**

Carl R Rogers, Columbus, OH: Charles E Merrill, 1969.

Yet another attempt to subvert the 'normal' practice of higher education, this book had a profound effect on a generation of practitioners and its message is still strong and clear today. (Note: we prefer this original 1969 edition to the updated version titled *Freedom to Learn for the 80s*, by the same publisher in 1983.) Heavy emphasis is placed on the key role of the learner and on the importance of allowing autonomy in and for learning. When its message is taken to heart, the effect can be disturbing and revolutionary. The case study *Goodies and Baddies* in our book shows the effect it had on one teacher who sought to change his approach to teaching after reading *Freedom to Learn* (and also highlights some of the difficulties which may be encountered when a teacher radically changes the normal approach to teaching and learning). Rogers' book remains a powerful articulation of reasons why teaching and learning should be directed towards empowering students to learn and to become active, autonomous, thinking and feeling human beings.

- **Becoming Critical. Education, Knowledge and Action Research**

Wilfred Carr and Stephen Kemmis, London: Falmer Press, 1986.

Opinions vary about how difficult this book is to read but certainly some may find it hard going. However, if you want to be more rigorous in locating your own teaching theories, metaphors and practices within wider theories of knowledge, then this is the book for you. It eloquently outlines three distinct 'world views', those of: natural science (positivism), the interpretive view (phenomenology), and critical theory (especially with regard to Habermas). It is also an essential source for the theoretical foundations of action research and for the view that educational theory and practice should be viewed as one in the notion of *praxis*. For the educational specialist or developer it is essential reading.

- **Curriculum Action Research. A Handbook of Methods and Resources for the Reflective Practitioner**

James McKernan, London: Kogan Page, 1991.

You may have become convinced that you want to be a reflective practitioner, but how do you start? One answer to this is to investigate your own teaching and your students' learning using action research (action inquiry) methods. Action research is the current vogue in educational research and is a perspective which encourages teachers to inquire actively into what they are doing in the classroom, whether it is working, and what they can do to improve it. Teachers can gain much from this kind of systematic inquiry without need for the control groups and quasi-experimental methods which for so long dominated classroom research, to such little effect. It could be argued that every teacher as a responsible professional *should* continually be engaged in action research on his or her own teaching. McKernan's book outlines approaches to action research and offers a vast number of suggestions for collecting action research materials. There are good possibilities for publishing inquiries of this nature in educational or subject/educational journals. For some this might provide an extra stimulus to conduct research and development programmes on their own teaching.

- **Zen and the Art of Motorcycle Maintenance: An Inquiry into Values**

Robert M Pirsig, London: Corgi, 1976.

This cult classic attained worldwide recognition after being quoted by all sorts of thinkers and scholars as an 'important' book. Apart from asking some fundamental questions about the way we live our lives, it is actually a very good read, too. There are many references to the way we conceive of education, which have a direct bearing on practice and policy. In essence much of the book tries to tease out what we mean by 'quality' – a word which has been much bandied about in higher education recently. There is also an interesting episode where the teacher in the book tells his students at the beginning of a course that they have all passed and asks what they would like to do now. Is it perhaps another case study in the making?

- **The Times Higher Education Supplement**
Published weekly by The Times Supplements Ltd, Priory House, St John's Lane, London EC1M 4BX.

- **Campus**
Published weekly by Australian Campus Review Weekly, Locked Bag 19, Paddington, New South Wales 2021.

- **The Chronicle of Higher Education**
Published weekly at 1255 Twenty-Third Street, NW, Washington, DC 20037.

Reflective practice and the everyday 'nitty-gritty' of teaching practice do not occur in a vacuum. The named newspapers help practitioners to keep abreast of the political, economic, intellectual, social and institutional movements which affect the climate in which we teach. At least that is why some of us read them; the rest of us are looking for jobs in the advertisement sections. Many teachers may well know of these publications, but we have been surprised to find that quite a number of academics do not, and this is the reason for their appearance here. *The Higher* as it is now styled remains the major quality paper of higher education in the UK and related areas of the world. It also has the distinct advantage of the inspired back page satire of Laurie Taylor. *Campus* is a relative newcomer directed at the Australasian market and it provides useful information and comment with regard to that part of the world. *The Chronicle of Higher Education* is the main American contender in this field.

Appendix: The Use of Teaching Case Studies in Seminars for Staff Development

Introduction

The original use of the case studies included in this book was as resources for seminar series where teachers in higher education come together to consider cases which they and their colleagues present and which lead them to examine many important issues which have arisen in their experiences of teaching. In this appendix, we summarize our approach for the benefit of those who might wish to use our cases or their own in a similar fashion.

We envisage that such seminar series would be organized by educational development units or similar agencies, and these notes should give such units enough information to enable them to run a seminar series in a manner similar to our own. Additional details are available from the authors on request; see page 159 for the address.

Our programme usually comprises eight seminar sessions per series, with each session lasting two hours. We accept enrolments on a 'first come' basis. We limit the number of participants to 14 per series but have found it advisable to accept 16, which allows for a couple of people to drop out.

The participants receive Part One of the first case to be discussed in the series together with a reading (see below) at least a week before the first session. Part Two (and other parts if necessary) of the case for week one are photocopied and kept ready for distribution; so too are Part One of the case for the next week and the reading for the next week. These are distributed at the end of the first session.

Process of the first and subsequent sessions

A. Opening

Having tried a number of devices for starting off a seminar series, we have settled for the following pattern. Participants are met and welcomed as they enter the room for the first time and find places at tables arranged in a circle so that every participant can see everyone else. One of the seminar leaders, whom we will call the chairperson, then opens proceedings by outlining what will happen during the session, as follows:

- We will introduce ourselves to each other.
- We will break into groups of about four for initial discussion of some of the highlights of Part One of the case for approximately 15 minutes.
- We will then re-convene and discuss what has come out of the small groups for about 40 minutes.
- We will then pass around copies of Part Two of the case before breaking for coffee (approximately 15–20 minutes for the first session, ten minutes at subsequent sessions).
- After re-convening we will discuss Part Two (and other parts if applicable) for about 30 minutes.
- The final 15 minutes will be used for discussion of the reading, for introducing a current personal situation, and for distributing the case and reading for next week.

After the round of introductions and the identification of some of the highlights of Part One of the case by the small groups, the chairperson starts the full group discussion with an open-ended question such as one of the following: 'What is happening in this case? What is going on here? What do you make of this case? What do you think about all this?' In the weeks that follow, we generally throw open the question as to whether participants wish to form small groups as an activity preliminary to the whole group discussion. They will commonly opt to do so for two or three weeks until they feel completely comfortable in the large group setting, after which they tend to prefer to go straight into the large group discussion.

B. Part One

Full group discussion now commences on the case. There may be some reluctance, however, on the part of participants to speak out. If there is silence, we generally prefer to leave this uninterrupted for a considerable time before intervening. If an intervention becomes necessary, we would try to ensure that this is directed towards releasing the tension and nervousness which has grown, rather than towards the actual question posed. In the first week there may be long silences between contributions made by individuals. It is imperative that the seminar leaders do not jump into these spaces and feel responsible for keeping the dialogue going. Discussion will become easier as the session progresses and as the series as a whole develops.

Towards the halfway point in the session, which is used as a break for coffee, the chairperson will intervene and ask participants to state what they think was the next thing to happen in the case. This is usually effected by each person venturing an opinion in turn. It may also be effective to ask participants to state not only what they think *did* happen, but also to say what they think *should* have happened, what should have been done. The device of getting participants to commit themselves on these two questions is useful for provoking interest in the next part of the case and subsequent discussion. At the completion of the round, the chairperson then distributes Part Two of the case, and the group breaks for coffee.

C. Part Two

When the group re-convenes after the break, the chairperson may start off the discussion with questions such as: 'What did you make of the second part of the case? What do you think about what happened? Did what happened surprise you? Have you changed your mind about what is going on here?' Generally, discussion of the Part Two case is easier to initiate and tends to be quite easily self-sustaining and at times boisterous. As the last 15 minutes of the session approach, the chairman must decide whether or not to try formally to tie up the case. In the early sessions it may be beneficial for the self-confidence of the group members if the chairperson runs through the main issues that he or she thought were of importance and which were identified prior to the meeting. Invariably, nearly every point raised will have been covered by the group, usually in considerable detail. In our experience, therefore, as the seminar series develops, it is not always necessary for the chairperson or group to recap the case.

D. Closing

The practice that has developed during our own experience of running seminar series is to leave the last 15 minutes of the session completely free. In this period, participants may care to comment upon the reading for that week, or upon something that is currently happening with them. The latter has been the most popular, with many and varied problem situations currently being faced by individuals in teaching or in relationships with students having been raised. Other group members sometimes offer advice on these occasions, and the individuals concerned usually report back to the group as the situation unfolds or is resolved.

This then is the general process followed in the first and subsequent seminar sessions. It will be appreciated that the part played by the seminar leaders is important to the success of the process. With this in mind, we now consider this topic in more detail.

Seminar leaders

We have found that there are many advantages in having two leaders participating throughout a seminar series. For the first and even the second series organized, it is quite reassuring to have a colleague present when one is unsure of how successful the discussion will be, and how well one will manage an essentially open-ended process. The main reason for having two leaders goes further than simply providing mutual support, however.

In most group-based educational activities there are two principal roles which need to be played. First, there is a need for organization – of the seminar series itself and of the process followed by the group. Someone needs to start proceedings off, suggest using smaller groups where appropriate, draw each segment to a close and generally manage time so that it is used efficiently and in accordance with the wishes of the group as a whole.

The role taken by this person is essentially one of facilitation. There may be a need to ask participants to clarify or expand on points which they have raised and to confront contradiction or confusion that may have emerged. It is also important that opinions are sought from those who have not yet spoken, and that those who may wish to speak, but are finding it difficult, should be assisted. In light of this, it may occasionally be necessary to curb the more outspoken participants. Participants should also be reminded of the need to examine cases from the viewpoints of both teachers and students. Finally, there are questions as to how the feelings of the group can be brought out and how the valuing of individuals and the creation of a climate of trust and respect can be accomplished. None of this requires a substantial amount of 'subject', 'content' or 'expert' knowledge. The role has been called that of being 'in authority' rather than 'an authority'. In terms of Heron's (1989) six dimensions of facilitation, it includes the planning, structuring, feeling and valuing dimensions. In our seminar series, the person designated to take this role is called the chairperson.

The other leader in our seminars is called the 'educator'. This person takes the second role, as 'an authority' and as such can venture opinions and information from a background and experience in the philosophy, theory and practice of education. This is obviously a role with many dangers. If it is played wrongly, the educator may be seen as the arbiter of 'truth' or as the final authority on issues which arise during the case discussions. However, when the role is played carefully, the educator can introduce insights and experiences to broaden or deepen the discussion, while at the same time avoiding taking over or putting an authoritative end to the discussion. Without this role being played, it is possible that the discussion could devolve into a cosy occasion for the parading of prejudices. The educator can stop this happening, by asking that views of human nature and the practice of education be subjected to critical scrutiny. As such, the educator fills the meaning and confronting dimensions of Heron's (1989) six dimensions of facilitation. This should be done by the educator speaking 'within the case', however, rather than from 'outside' knowledge and research.

The role of the educator is likely to be more confrontational and controversial than that of the chairperson. The separation of the two roles thus has the advantage of focusing disagreement, confrontation and controversy on a person other than the chairperson. Any negative feelings which may arise in the group are not, therefore, attached to the chairperson or to the seminar series itself. The chairperson may thus remain everyone's friend and may value and encourage each participant, as the threat of the chairperson alienating a particular participant is greatly reduced.

In practice the roles of the two seminar leaders may be somewhat more intertwined than has been indicated so far. Thus, every so often the chairperson may venture a personal anecdote or experience or offer an insight which displays his or her own analysis and value position on the case. Similarly, the educator may play a facilitating role in terms of the group process, by helping in the feeling and valuing dimensions of facilitation, for example. It is therefore worthwhile for both seminar leaders to have reasonable general facilitation skills, and books such as those by Heron (1989) and Boud (1987) are valuable resources in this respect.

Discussion content

So far we have provided information on the process of running the seminars. We shall deal with the important issue of the content of discussion only briefly here because we identify both general and specific issues for consideration in the introduction to this book and in the discussion which accompanies each case study. Organizers of seminar series should consult these sections for suggestions about questions and issues for discussion, but we repeat that our lists should not be taken as either exhaustive or definitive. We recommend that discussion be initiated in as open-ended and general a fashion as possible and that the participants themselves be allowed to define the issues for consideration.

We use pre-existing case studies for only the early seminars in our series. Because case studies generated by the participants in the current seminars can be seen to be immediately relevant, they heighten interest in the proceedings and we use such newly-generated cases extensively.

Developing and managing current cases

In the first publicity to be sent out we make it clear that we hope each participant in a seminar series will construct his or her own case. We mention this again at the end of the first session and at the end of each succeeding session. By about the fourth week of the series, participants have a fair idea of the form that a case should take, and many will have thought of a topic, even though they may not have written the case yet. From this point on, we will start introducing cases written by participants in the present seminar series, depending only upon how many cases are brought forward and how quickly. We would recommend that between two and four of the last weeks of the seminar series be devoted to such cases.

Our main guideline for the development of a case is that it should refer to some 'real life' incident which the writer has experienced, or of which he or she has direct, first-hand knowledge. In addition, each case should have at least two parts and some decision as to what action should next be taken has to be made at the end of Part One.

The process for discussing newly-produced cases follows that described for the early cases in the seminar series, with one major difference. We suggest a ground rule that the case be discussed as though the person who wrote it were not there, and he or she should not participate in the discussion until about three-quarters of the way through. We have found this to be a useful device to stop the case author continually trying to justify positions and actions taken, and by so doing unduly influencing and restricting the discussion. The case is thus discussed in depth by the other participants in just the same way as a pre-existing case, with participants having to make interpretations solely from the evidence in front of them. When the case writer is invited to contribute to the discussion, he or she will almost certainly want to clarify and re-interpret things going on in the case, but at least now the discussion will have had a chance to range widely, unconstrained by possible rationalizations and self-justifications by the author.

Although the consideration by the rest of the group may have difficult moments for the case author, the spirit of cohesion and mutual respect fostered in the group up to this time should prevent criticism being made vindictively. Also, the fact that other participants will be in the same situation can only help this cause. Finally, it is perhaps worth pointing out that we have never felt it necessary to intervene in a current case session because of the possibility of criticism being carried too far.

Readings

At the end of each session we not only distribute the Part One case for the next session, but we also make available a reading for the following week. The readings have been deliberately chosen as being 'light,' interesting and stimulating for the 'non-educationalists' who attend our seminar series. We have specifically left out papers directed more towards the specialist in higher education, together with those advocating particular brands of learning theory or educational psychology. Several of the items listed in our annotated bibliography were sources for some of our readings, but others are equally suitable. All of our experience suggests caution, however, in terms of the length, style and content of the articles selected.

The readings which we use are not selected to supplement particular cases *per se*. They are for general enjoyment, to stimulate interest and to widen horizons, rather than to augment specific case discussions. Choosing readings to augment a case could unduly influence and restrict discussion by pointing to a 'correct' interpretation or suggesting a 'right' answer. This is not to say that the readings we have used are in some sense 'neutral' – they are not, but neither are they restricted to confirming our own beliefs. Although we would profoundly agree with some of the readings, we would also, individually, disagree with others.

We have indicated that we do not tend to spend much time discussing readings in the case sessions. This is because our participants have usually chosen, for the final segment of the meeting, to speak more about current situations facing them than about the readings. On the other hand, information and questions originating in the readings have been introduced into case sessions by some participants, while others have had detailed discussions with us personally about particular readings.

A specimen series

The case studies included in this book will promote discussion of a wide variety of problems faced by teachers, and organizers of seminars may wish to look through the selection and choose case studies which are appropriate for their own circumstances. For a first run of a seminar series, however, we could recommend a possible sequence based on our experience. On the assumption that a series of eight seminars has been decided upon, we would suggest the following. (See the individual case studies for indications of the issues raised.)

Session 1 – Too Much 'Glasnost' in the Classroom?
Session 2 – The 'A' versus 'D' Project
Session 3 – Blue Moves *and* Just Desserts (both cases in the one session)
Session 4 – Goodies and Baddies
Session 5 – Did She or Did She Not? *and* The Discontented Student (both cases)
Sessions 6, 7 and 8 – cases prepared by your own participants.

Finally, we invite you to write to us at the address below with any questions or comments you might have about the cases or their use in seminars for staff development. We also send our best wishes for the success of your seminar series and are confident that, like us, you and many staff within your institution will derive much value from considering the case studies in this book as well as those which you construct and interpret yourselves.

Peter Schwartz and Graham Webb
University of Otago
Higher Education Development Centre
Box 56
Dunedin
New Zealand

References

Boud, D (1987) 'A facilitator's view of adult learning', in Boud, D and Griffin, V (eds) *Appreciating Adults Learning: From the Learner's Perspective*, London: Kogan Page.
Heron, J (1989) *The Facilitator's Handbook*, London: Kogan Page; East Brunswick, New Jersey: Nichols Publishing.

Subject Index